YOUR FLOATERS

Essentials for Happiness

K.B. Trehan

PUSTAK MAHAL®

Published by

Pustak Mahal®, Delhi
J-3/16, Daryaganj, New Delhi-110002
☎ 23276539, 23272783, 23272784 • *Fax:* 011-23260518
E-mail: info@pustakmahal.com • *Website:* www.pustakmahal.com

Sales Centre
10-B, Netaji Subhash Marg, Daryaganj, New Delhi-110002
☎ 23268292, 23268293, 23279900 • *Fax:* 011-23280567
E-mail: rapidexdelhi@indiatimes.com

• Hind Pustak Bhawan
6686, Khari Baoli, Delhi-110006
☎ 23944314, 23911979

Branch Offices
Bengaluru: ☎ 22234025 • *Telefax:* 22240209
E-mail: pustak@airtelmail.in • pustak@sancharnet.in
Mumbai: ☎ 22010941
E-mail: rapidex@bom5.vsnl.net.in
Patna: ☎ 3294193 • *Telefax:* 0612-2302719
E-mail: rapidexptn@rediffmail.com
Hyderabad: *Telefax:* 040-24737290
E-mail: pustakmahalhyd@yahoo.co.in

© Copyright : **Author**

ISBN 978-81-223-1269-0
Edition : 2012

The Copyright of this book, as well as all matter contained herein (including pictures) rests with the Publishers. No person shall copy the name of the book, its title design, matter, illustrations & photographs in any form and in any language, totally or partially or in any distorted form. Anybody doing so shall face legal action and will be responsible for damages.

Printed at : Param Offsetters, Okhla, New Delhi-110020

Contents

Acknowledgements 5
Editor's Note 6
Author's Note 7
When I looked Within: Know thyself 9
Learning to Unlearn 25
God Makes You.
You Make Your Attitude 41
Never give up 51
This too Shall Pass 61
Mind Over Matter 67
Focus Your Energy 87
He who enjoys his Work,
never works a day in his Life 99
Ego & Me 109
The Art of Giving 123
Fume-mitigation
Managing Anger 141
Forgiveness 153
It comes back 167
Reshape ... Remake Yourself 177
Accept Life as it Comes 189
Ultimate Relationship 201

❝ To live is to change
and
to be perfect
is to have changed often. ❞

— *John Henry Newman*

Acknowledgements

- to the Almighty for His continuous advice, guidance and blessings;

- to my family members, especially my loving children and grand children for their love and support;

- to all my relations and friends for illuminating my mind by sharing their experiences;

- to M/s Ram Avtar Gupta and Rohit Gupta for their valuable inputs and cooperation in making it possible; and

- to all my readers, with a wish & prayer for their wonderful life ahead.

Editor's Note

It is amazing how destiny unfolds and new chapters, new people add new dimensions to our world. It was a fateful meeting with "the man with a silver head" (the words that ringed first in my head when I met Mr KB Trehan) that appended an enduring association with the author. Today, after experiencing three of his books (especially the sensitive semi-fiction *Dancing on the Notes of Life*) and numerous interactions hence, I know for sure that the man with a silver head has a truly golden heart – very seldom does one get a chance to interact with someone as versatile and thoughtful. Moreover, I find it extraordinary when an editorial project invigorates and triggers an internal dialogue and perhaps, an inner evolution. This opportunity is unique. I am thankful and positive that a substantial contribution to the life of everyone who reads this book will be made.

There are sixteen floaters/chapters in the book and I am positive that at any given point in time and space, at least 10 aspects would be of value to any reader.

It is recommended that until you have mastered and tamed the waves of this ocean called life – *Don't Forget Your Floaters*, the book that you hold in your hands can serve as a manual to the young and an eye opener for the mature. Every page, every chapter is an entry point to the 'new' wise life that you are about to begin. My advice would be that one should not read this book cover to cover, but one floater/chapter at a time. Read it to improve your understanding of life and more importantly, of yourself. And if you think, you are a great swimmer who has managed to swim to the horizon every time – share with us your secret/your floater. Remember, you are the medium and you are message of your life.

Wishing you happy floating, perhaps sailing through a very wonderful, exciting and meaningful life.

Charushilla Narula
charushilla@gmail.cam

Author's Note

One of my most quoted lines and possibly one of the key messages of this book is that the best place to find a helping hand is at the end of your own arm. Going through the aisles of our lives, we come across a number of obstacles, problems, hurdles, challenges, sorrows and tragedies. No matter how open or closed we keep our minds, in reality, each moment teaches us something invaluable. We all become products of our experiences and the reactions thereof… Incidents in my own life and of my friends, relatives and colleagues have become the basis of my learning and given me a deeper insight into the mysteries of this ocean called "life".

I would be an absolute egoist if I declared that I have deciphered the secret to happiness. And then again, the hypothesis is not that people's lives are a series of 'should haves' and 'could haves'; but, I have yet to come across anyone who has never thought – what if I could live all over again?

Would I not want to do things a little differently? Manage my ego at work and in my relationships? Develop assertiveness skills? Be able to forgive effortlessly and give selflessly? Tame my anger…,etc. I call them "floaters" and I strongly believe that it is never too late to use them.

What has become crystal clear to me is that while all these aspects belong to our outer being and may seem utopion at first look, but, it is only by deeper introspection, that we can really expand our life and make it happier; or "enter the good life."

This book, which is armed with a good set of floaters, can truly expand the parameters of your life, explore hidden treasures to live a large contended happy life.

Don't Forget Your Floaters – Essentials for Happiness uses actual incidents and life situations to reach out to the reader's sensibilities.

I am thankful to Arvind Bharadwaj, the editor of my book, *Illusions of Love*, who helped me etch the initial draft for this book. He also introduced me to Charushilla, a conscientious literary consultant and an editor with exceptional communication acumen. She rendered her full help to give the book its final character and shape.

Before I hand you over your floaters, dear reader, I want you to believe that:

i. every human being can change his life by altering his way of thinking & attitude; and

ii. never quit learning. Learning is a continuous process and one can learn much from the varied experiences of others and put them to use to make life smoother & happier.

Together, let's enter the good life..........

God Bless.

[Chapter One]

When I looked Within: Know thyself

Observe all men, thyself most.

– *Benjamin Franklin*

Be able to be alone. Lose not the advantage of solitude, and the society of thyself.

– *Thomas Browne*

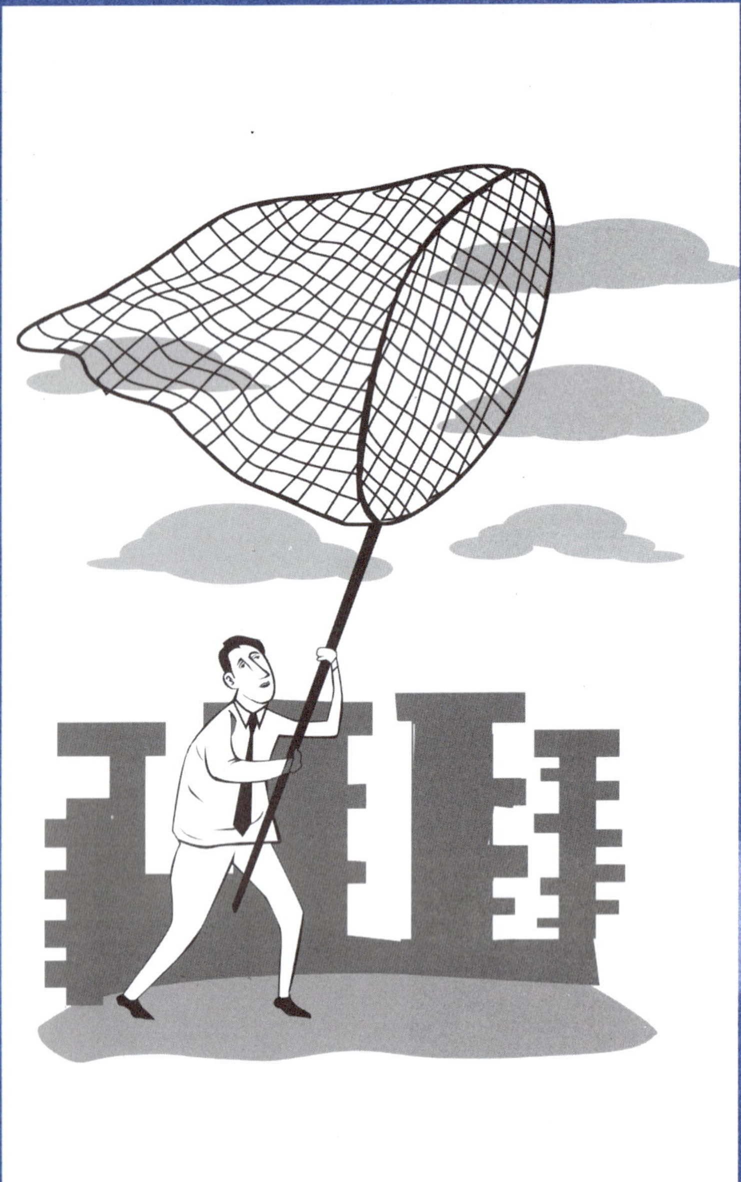

When I looked Within: Know thyself ■ 11

You wake up every day. Possibly, in the same house, the same room, the same bed. Then why is it that some days you feel really upbeat – you are ready to conquer anything, while on some other days you curse the morning – gloom and burden of life surmounts your being. You blame your condition to the environment that surrounds you – the demanding boss, the cranky child, the nagging mother-in-law, the promotion, the movie, the new dress, the weather…the list is endless!

For the sake of understanding, let us suppose that I had the desire to climb a mountain. Now just the thought of climbing a mountain might fill me with energy and enthusiasm, but will not really give happiness. Also enroute, the climb will have hurdles, pain and difficulties, which in no case can be synonymous with happiness. Still I undertake the challenge. So, obviously, when I reach the summit, I feel happy!

Now while I was in the ordeal of climbing the mountain, what was I seeking? Was it really happiness? (I could have been happy and a lot more comfortable sitting at home.) It was just fatigue and struggle that I felt during the climb.

Also, what are the feelings later? Upon climbing the mountain, I became happy. But will this happiness last for ever? It will be there for some time, along with the sense of achievement, and then it will slowly abate and disappear… and then what?

The point is: it is not really happiness alone that we seek. For if it was so, once happiness came to us in some way or the other, we would be happy forever. What we find in life is that one day we are happy because of something or someone, and the next day the happiness is no longer there! And then we again go about seeking it in some other way!

This seek, this chase is like trying to catch a cloud. You will never really get anything in your hands.

In other words, fulfillment of desires does not bring permanent happiness. Desires are never ending. One quickly replaces the other! And the happiness that accompanies does not last. Soon, one starts to think that one will surely get everlasting happiness by the fulfillment of some other desire. This vicious cycle never ends and one remains trapped in it for life unto death.

Therefore, our search should be essentially for everlasting and permanent happiness. But how?

Know thyself, said the Greek philosopher Plato, for by knowing oneself one can open up innumerable doors of possibilities in life.

Remember: Knowing oneself is knowing what we want in life!

We may be highly qualified, we may be earning well, but unless we understand ourselves – who we are from the inside, we will never feel fulfilled and happy.

What do we want?

What do we seek?

What is our goal?

Do we want peace? Do we want happiness or some sort of gratification, which would give us happiness? Or do we want status, money or authority?

Are we clear? Is there clarity in our mind? Possibly, we do not know ourselves what exactly we want. Before we search for peace, happiness, god, etc., let us know ourselves first.

Knowing the self is the highest journey that a human can undertake, for it opens the doors to calmness, peace and tranquility, as a result of which true and lasting joy automatically flows into one's being. Without the key of self-awareness, all our living-by-the-law efforts like visiting shrines, listening to spiritual discourses, reading holy texts will not only go waste, but also keep us trapped in the cycle of happiness and sorrow.

The real attainment of true and lasting happiness can come only by knowing the self. This attainment has to come through oneself alone and it cannot be given to us by anyone or anything. It is ultimately the society of thy own self that shall open the gates of heaven for you!

Knowing oneself also accentuates a very important part of our self, and that is the ability to intuit, to perceive, to mystically know what lies ahead...sometimes even through our dreams!

Inner Voice to the Rescue

2005: I was scheduled to fly off to Dubai for a very important meeting. This was not the first time I was making a trip even when I knew that my wife was unwell. She had been in that condition for long now. There was no reason to be worried, but all of a sudden at the last moment I had a change of mind and I cancelled my journey. Later fhat day, the condition of my wife deteriorated and she passed away. I could be with her when she breathed her last...just because I chose to listen to my inner voice and did, as it said.

Since that day, I became deeply interested in the power within, which is available to us all the time. It is up to us to establish relationship with this divine strength. It speaks to us in times of need. We should develop the capacity to listen to it. To benefit from this process, we need to be very alert and have self awareness.

I interacted with a number of people in this regard and came to know about their experiences. I concluded:

The inner voice is NOT a 'special gift' that only a few people (the clairvoyant) are endowed with. The inner voice speaks to each individual. The special aspect is to be able to listen to it, obey it and regard it. Do not ignore it. This is a very

> Everyone who wills can hear the inner voice. It is within everyone
> — *Mahatma Gandhi*

big resource and must be effectively managed and not wasted. All of us have the capability and potential to connect to it.

Now this inner voice or the power within that provides solutions to problems, that shows us the way in confusing times or inspires and motivates us, need not always manifest as a voice whispering in one's mind! It could give its verdict or its perspective in the form of some feeling or idea, rather than words.

The German chemist Friedrich August von Kekule was trying to crack the shape of the Benzene atom. He had been working hard for many months, without any breakthrough. Then one day, while working on the same problem, he dozed off in his chair. Suddenly, in a dream he saw atoms seemingly made of light moving round in a circle. Next moment, the circle of atoms was replaced by a snake that moved round and round in a perfect circle. At last, the snake held its own tail in its mouth and continued to whirl in the form of a circle.

Kekule woke up the next moment with the image of the snake still clear in his mind. It did not take him long to realize that out of his sub-consciousness had appeared the solution to the problem that he had been trying to crack. The structure of Benzene was a ring! He had tried all structures and this was one shape he had not thought of before!

Dreams have inspired many people over the ages to take to a particular way or to adopt some approach. If not all, at least some dreams are nothing but the inner voice trying to communicate some important message in a different way. This could happen when the conscious mind is too preoccupied or confused to catch the subtle and silent directions of the inner power. During sleep, the conscious mind is lulled into inactivity and at that time, the subconscious mind or the inner power is free to communicate its message which the sleeper visualizes as a dream. So dream on dear readers…

Progress towards our Inner Self

Primary progress towards becoming aware of our inner voice happens through the path of prayer. Prayer is the acceptance of what is happening in this world. It is not the problems of our life that disturb us. It is the agitation of our mind that makes us fearful. Praying is an attitude towards life, the attitude of accepting things as they are and not being disturbed by them. This attitude grants us the strength to remain composed in every situation.

The biggest argument in favour of prayer is that it relieves the mind of anxiety, worry and tension, which are normal companions of life. Life is not all sweet. It also has pain, suffering, worry and failures. Prayer helps us keep up our spirits high in challenging and difficult situations. Simultaneously, prayer has great corrective powers too and the capacity to bring happiness in life.

The words of a Zen master echo in my mind: "Sit down and be calm in the mind! First, stop the storm going on in your mind and then you will find that your will becomes the same as His will and you will never be agitated by anything."

The Seat of God

Even before prayer, we should be clear where actually that Supreme Power resides. If the phone number you have in your mind is wrong, you cannot talk to the person you want to, even if you have a phone and a connection. If you do not have the right address, you cannot expect your letters to be delivered to the right person. Similarly, knowing where God is, is the first step towards utilizing the power of prayer.

Fact is that the divine force that does good for all mankind is hidden in us. The biggest mistake we make is in presuming that it is seated somewhere far from us, up in the sky somewhere or in heaven.

> *In the Bhagwad Gita (15.15), Lord Krishna says – "I am seated in everyones heart ..." Here Krishna speaks for the Supreme Godhead when he uses the word "I".*
> *In yet another verse (10.20), he repeats this very fact – "I am the Super soul, O Arjun, seated in the hearts of all living entities..."*

The Bible too reveals this fact in the following words –

'Know you not that you are the temple of God, and the spirit of God dwells in you." (First Corinthians 3:16 King James Translation)

Prayer thus should always be directed at the Supreme Force, also called the Self, residing within.

> Kingdom of heaven is within us. – Jesus

In that Heaven, God dwells. He is therefore within us.

> Kasturi Kundal Base, Mrig Dhoonde Ban Maahi
> *(The musk deer wanders through the forest trying to search for the source of musk fragrance knowing not that it is in its own navel.)*
> Aise Tere Ram Hain, Par Tu Jaane Naahi!
> *(Likewise, God dwells in you O man and you know not!)* – Kabir

God is living within us and is seated in our hearts. This is the first thing we should understand and believe in. Otherwise, our very act of praying would go futile. So, whenever one prays, one should visualize Him seated in the heart.

People also believe that God lives in temples or churches or gurudwaras or any other shrine. These are places of worship that are built with the purpose of providing a suitable place away from the hullabaloo of the world where one could sit in peace and offer prayers. The calmness in shrines helps one to attain silence and concentration of the mind.

How to pray

"That prayer is perfect, in which he, who is praying, remembers not that he is praying"

Praying is not just any act! It is first and foremost an act of faith. It is the display of faith that there is a higher power that rules life. So, even before one enters into the act of praying, one should nurture deep faith in the presence of God and in His omnipotence.

Development of faith is the primary prerequisite of tapping into the power of prayer. As someone once said, *"Faith is deliberate confidence in the character of God whose ways you may not understand at that time."* You may not understand life and what is happening in it. Your mind might baulk at certain events taking place in your life. Your thoughts may tell you that there is something wrong that is going on. But faith tells you that 'All is well' because the reins of your life are in the hands of the Supreme Master.

Many people say that we remember God only when we are in trouble. I believe this is really not true. When we find ourselves in a difficult situation, the first thing we tend to do is use our own intelligence, our own mind to get out of the situation. We show more faith in "our wisdom". Only when everything else fails, we turn to God. If only we learnt to directly present all our problems to the Supreme Power, we would find solutions much faster and in an easier manner.

Therefore, we need to constantly remember that there is a Supreme Power to whom we can turn. The mind simply forgets. To keep it always in a state of remembrance, there are many ways. The sages of yore suggested the way of 'chanting of God's name'.

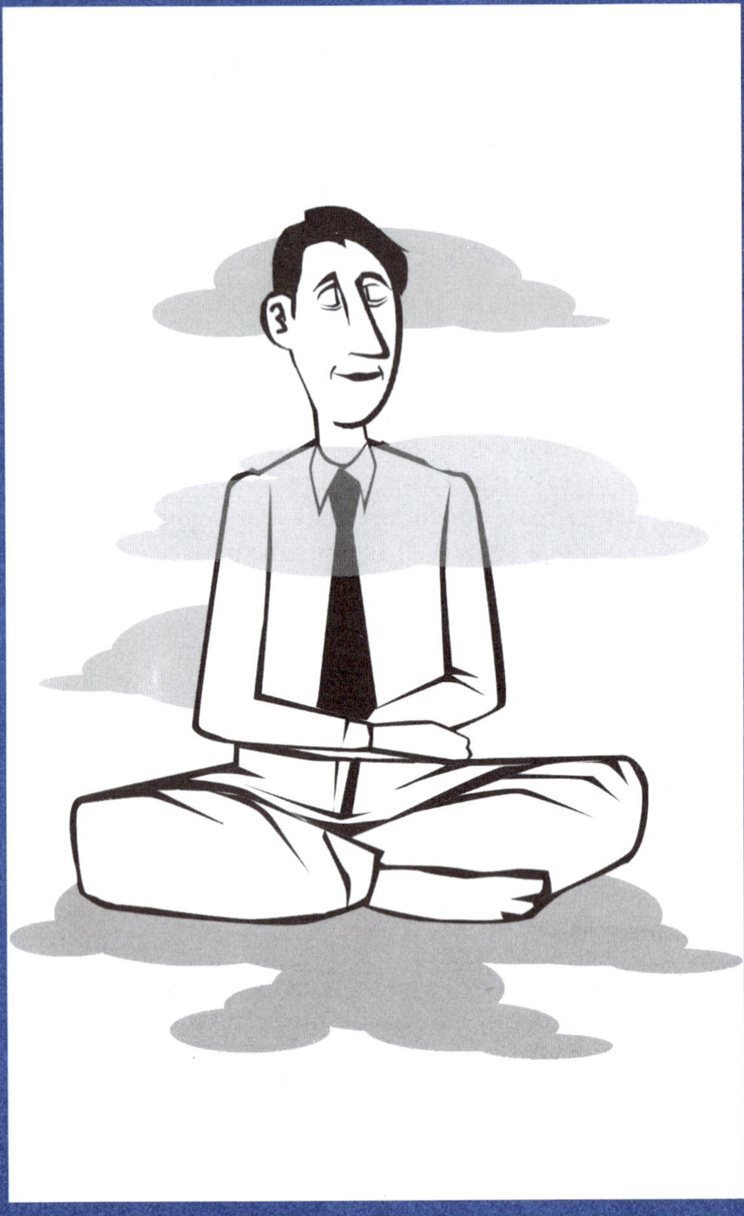

Chanting is a very powerful tool to reach Him. By keeping His all-powerful name on the tongue, we feel very near to God.

Chanting can be done in many ways. In the beginning, a person is advised to chant out loud a certain number of times every day, at a fixed time and in a fixed number. That is just to make the name of God etched firmly in the mind. Later, one should move on to what is called *Ajapa Jaap*, or chanting without keeping a count and all the time or whenever one has time. This type of chanting is done in the mind and making a habit of speaking out God's name silently all the time helps the mind to easily remember the Supreme Power.

Another important aspect of praying is learning to relax and sit in silence at some place all alone. It is always best to be alone while offering prayers. The holy scripture Bible says;

> *When you pray, do not be like the hypocrites, for they love to pray standing in the synagogues and on the street corners to be seen by men. I tell you the truth, they have received their reward in full. But when you pray, go into your room, close the doors and pray to your Father, who is unseen. Then your Father, who sees what is done in secret, will reward you.* (Matthew 6:5-6).

By doing so, we communicate with Him and establish a direct relationship. God, who is living within us, listens to our prayer, responds to it and gives us the required advice and strength. In silence, our mind becomes still and then, we can listen to the subtle inner voice,

Sitting in silence is really like tuning in with the Supreme Channel.

> 66 We need to find God, and he cannot be found in noise and restlessness. God is the friend of silence. See how nature – trees, flowers, grass – grows in silence; see the stars, the moon and the sun, how they move in silence...We need silence to be able to touch souls. 99 — Mother Teresa

The act of praying itself can have two aspects – one is saying something to God, and the other is sitting in silence and trying to listen to the voice from within. When you sit down to pray or meditate, just say what you have to! But then be silent. In silence, the Inner Power communicates with you. God speaks in silence and listening in fact is the beginning of true prayer.

> Prayer is not merely an occasional impulse, to which we respond when we are in trouble; prayer is a life attitude.
> — Walter A. Mueller

This is a unique chapter which holds the key to a happier life and also a better understanding of the chapters that follow in this book. Therefore, to summarize the discussions presented above, first and foremost, it is essential to know the self, which happens as a consequence of our resolve to listen to our inner voice. Sharpening our ability to understand ourselves happens when we are able to connect to the Supreme Channel that resides within our own hearts.

The ways and means to connect to this Supreme Channel are through various methods of chanting, meditation and prayer.

To make a habit of sitting daily in silence and tuning into God, is the best way of keeping this channel of communication open and working. If we form this habit, we will find that solutions from within will keep pouring out regularly and one will not need to supplicate anymore.

"Trouble and perplexity drive me to prayer and prayer drives away perplexity and trouble." – Philip Melanchthen

Let us therefore learn to pray and establish a direct link and everlasting relationship with the Supreme Power that resides in our heart. And whatever we may do in life, let us remember –

> In happy moments, to praise God,
> In difficult moments, to seek God,
> In quiet moments, to listen to God,
> In painful moments, to trust God,
> And in every moment, to thank God.

[Chapter Two]

Learning to Unlearn

"The parents, the teachers, the neighbours, the friends – all are continuously giving a shape to your life, a style to your life. If you look into your mind you will find many voices together: your father is speaking, your grandfather is speaking, your mother, your brother, your teachers, your professors. But one thing you will not find there is your voice. Your voice has been completely repressed by other voices. Layer upon layer, you have lost track even of your own voice, of your own self, of your own face. So many masks..."

– *Osho*

My friend's wife greeted me at the door. "Uncle has come!" squealed the children.

"Hi, Uncle!"

I smiled at the seven-year-old princess and shook hands with the young lad of ten. They were a joyous pair.

Enters the grandmother. Undeterred by the spontaneous flow of happiness in the room, she promptly admonished the children for using the word 'Hi' and not touching my feet.

Solemnly and with forced obedience, the kids moved forward and bent over to 'get done' with the ritual. A look at the stern countenance of the grandmother told me that my words would go useless on her. She thought she knew best how her grandchildren should greet guests and that was it. In a private moment with the kids, they told me that they were expected to touch the feet of every guest.

It set me thinking.

Certain cultures within India teach children to express their respect and humility to their elders by way of touching their feet. But why?

Is the sentiment behind touching feet is to show respect for the elder or is it done because ritual demands it?

In present times are such gestures relevant?

What if the other person does not deserve such respect?

Should the children bow and touch feet of everyone against their will?

Conditioning of the mind, be it because of social values, religion, tradition or culture, prevents one from thinking rationally.

We enter this world with a clean slate. No definite thoughts of dos and don'ts. But as soon as we start understanding things, conditioning starts. Traditions, values, culture and the society expect us to behave in a certain manner. Many things that are imposed upon our unsullied mind seem irrational. But often our whys and protests are hushed and reprimanded with stern looks and harsh words. Do as you are told. Listen to your elders. At first reluctantly and then accepting it to be the order of things, we all give in. Over the years, this conditioning becomes so deep-rooted that the mind gets caught in a rut and is unable to rationalise or think logically.

Tradition or torture

One may call it tradition or culture or conditioning – most of us have accepted it because it helps us to smoothly sail through many hurdles of life, taking it as an anchor that gives some meaning to our existence. Have you ever wondered that it is the same tradition and its up-keep that results in an imposed sense of fear and guilt?

For example, even today in most parts of India, a married girl is expected to believe that her husband is God. The age-old advice continues – *"Jahan tumhari doli gayi hai, ab wahin se tumhari arthi niklegi"* (you have been wed to this family and you will leave only once you die.) No doubt things are now changing in many parts of urban India, but most of rural/traditional India still adheres to such thinking. The wife is expected to be servile and obedient. To serve her husband and obey him is her duty. And this attitude leads the unwitting bride to years of torture and pain in several instances.

☆ ☆ ☆

Preeti got married to a rich businessman. While bidding her goodbye, similar wise words of wifely duty were sermonised by her mother. The innocent girl took the advice verbatim, as an instruction coming from her own mother.

The very next day she got the shock of her life when she learnt that her husband was an alcoholic. He would not just start the day with alcohol, but at the slightest excuse, he would fly off his handle and start thrashing her. But separation or divorce was a taboo in her mind that had been conditioned by her parents. After a year, unable to take it any longer, Preeti decided to leave him. She went to her parents but they sent her back.

"You are married and your husband's house is your home and nothing more than that. You have to live there and bear with it."

"This is your fate as a girl," said her mother.

"You do not have a job. How will you survive in this world?" said her father with concern.

"Divorce is unheard of in our families," commented her elder brother. "Just keep serving him devotedly. With time, everything will be normal."

Preeti returned to her husband and for another one and a half years, she kept suffering in silence. She remained devoted as a wife, but that made no difference to her husband.

Then a day came when her husband beat her so mercilessly that she ran away. Her parents were still reluctant to file for divorce. At last, after six years of marriage, she got a divorce. One day in the court, her husband taunted her, "How will you survive without me?"

Her parents heard the comment and could say nothing for they too feared how their girl would fare in this harsh competitive world.

But Preeti proved everyone wrong. She went on to become a Chartered Accountant and soon a Company Secretary. Today, she is a very successful professional with a clientele that would make the best in the business envious.

☆ ☆ ☆

Conditioning of the mind, be it because of social values, religion, tradition or culture, prevents one from thinking rationally.

No parent would like to see their child beaten up and tortured. And yet, social norms prevented Preeti's parents to follow the rational course. "What will the people think if our daughter comes and lives with us? What will the society say if she gets divorced?" her parents thought.

Preeti proved that those who overcome the fear and restrictions imposed by tradition and culture ultimately come out triumphant. In other words, conditioning of the mind once overcome can open up a new world of opportunities, besides getting rid of many unfound fears, phobias and orthodox beliefs, leading to internal peace and happiness. .

Approval, acceptance and appreciation

Observe carefully. Our words and actions are driven by the deeply ingrained concepts of 'approval, acceptance and appreciation' of others, even if it means following the irrational course. And for this very reason, Preeti had to suffer for many extra years.

Such experiences can mentally shatter any sane person. When Preeti was beaten, she stood on the edge of a precipice. She could have thought of suicide, but fortunately she took the saner course. Besides, she did not let the views of others regarding her incapability of earning a living cloud her vision.

The fact is that every human being is born in a specific environment and that particular environment conditions him or her in one way or the other, leading to firm beliefs,

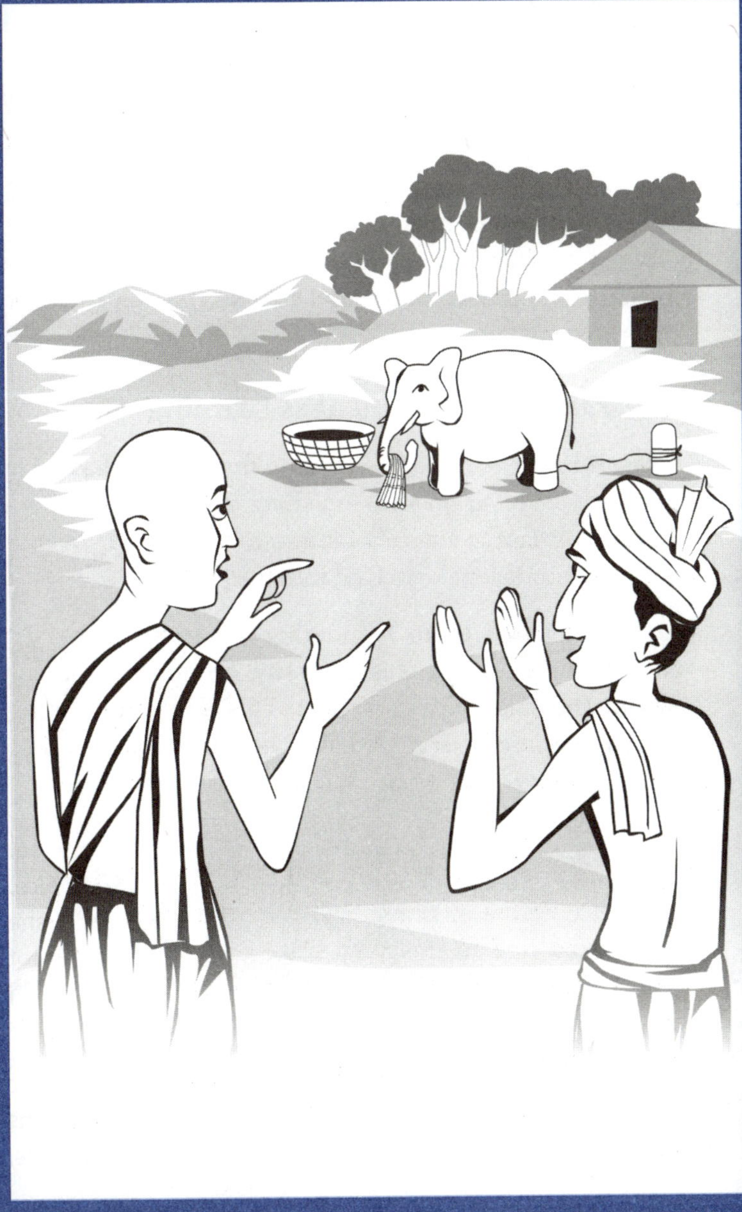

blind ideas and obsessions. This can be changed and corrected only by rational thinking and reasoning. It was thus that Preeti became free from her unfounded fears, phobias and beliefs. In other words, such a de-conditioning helps us to face the challenges of life, resulting in the emergence of a new, better and happier person than the one of the past.

Unlearning is as important as Learning

Once a Buddhist monk was passing through a village. He per chance came upon an astonishing sight: A fully grown elephant, in fact a virtual mammoth, was tied by a thin rope to a wooden stake driven into the ground.

The monk stood there wondering for some time. At last, unable to contain his curiosity, he approached the mahout and said, "My good man! This elephant is strong enough to uproot a large tree. And here he stands tied to a small wooden stake. What makes you so sure that he will not escape?"

The mahout laughed heartily and said, "Holy Sir! Lower your voice or the elephant will catch the idea. Actually, he has been tied to this very stake ever since he was a baby. At that time he did try his best to get free, but never succeeded. Now that experience fools him and he thinks he cannot free himself."

The monk stood there letting the words of the mahout sink in.

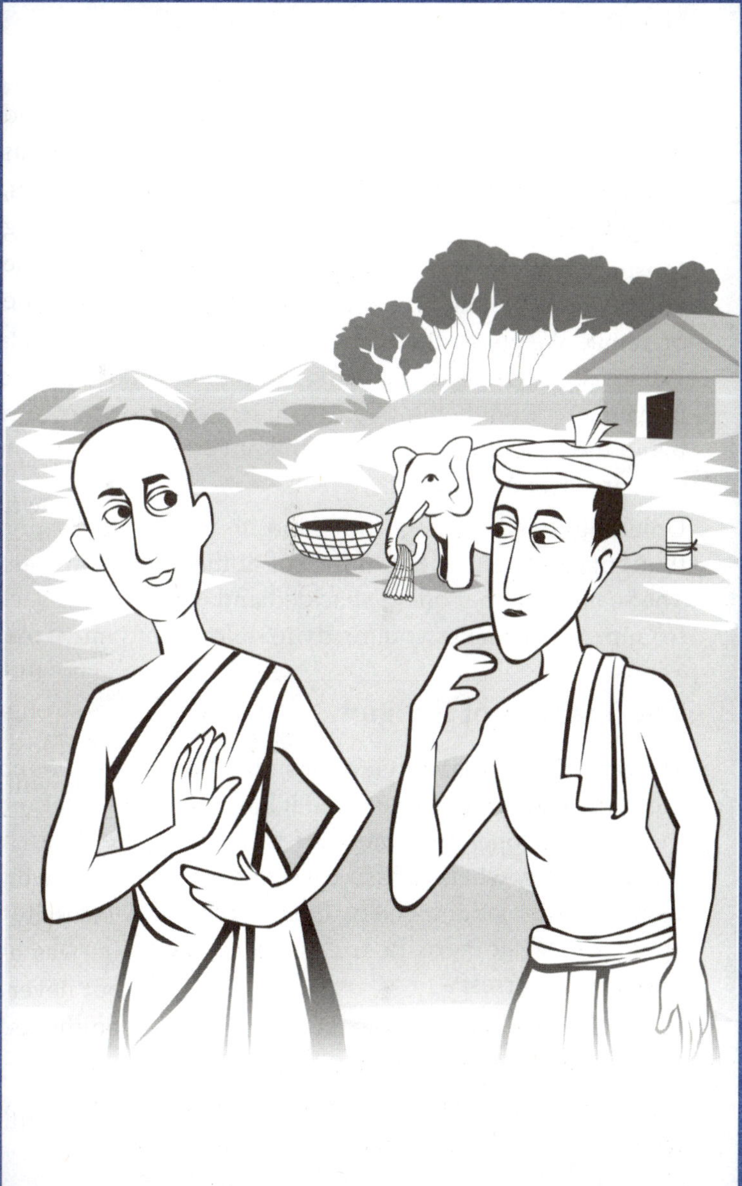

'Are we all not tied up mentally by similar weak ropes, which we think we cannot break free from?' he thought. The next moment the truth hit its mark and he became enlightened.

Most of us allow ourselves to be shackled by flimsy ropes all the time, in the name of tradition, culture, religion or habit. We think they are too strong for us to break. Whereas, the fact is that it is the mind that deludes us and prevents us from being free. If you feel tied down by any habit, thought or feeling, know it that you have the power to be free from it.

Unlearning is opening the mind to newer ideas and thoughts and getting out of the rut of the old and archaic. The realisation that one is shackled and is being held back from progress makes you, ready to unlearn and move on.

The Shackles of Religion

The orthodox Christian view was that the sun goes round the earth. Copernicus disproved it long ago, but was afraid to declare it openly because of the fear of the Church. Decades later, when Galileo tried to prove this fact to the world, he was condemned by the Church and was made to apologise. What more, he had to spend the rest of his life under house arrest!

When the first locomotive went on a trial run, people called it devil's iron beast riding in which one could go insane!

Religion talks about laws of nature and creation. So logically, its tenets should be rational and open to new ideas.

It will not be wrong to say that religion shackles us the most. Even the highly educated go on toeing the line without caring to stop and think. Let us take the example of making offerings in rivers in India.

The city drains and effluents from industries are sure to be blamed for the pollution of our rivers, but religious offerings like flowers, idols, etc are not making things any better. There are many rituals which prescribe that the worshipped material should be dispersed only in a river or pond. And we just wrap the material in polythene bags and swing them into rivers and ponds. Why do we continue to do so? Why? Is it because our gods would be displeased if we did not follow the religious dictates? What fails me is how the water-god, Varun, could be pleased when we keep polluting its bodies through such offerings?

A hair-raising instance of religious bigotry springs to my mind.

✯ ✯ ✯

Veena was diagnosed with juvenile diabetes at the age of ten. Ever since, she was on insulin. When she came of age, she was duly married into an affluent family that boasted of highly educated family members and a modern outlook towards life. When she stepped into her husband's house, Veena found that they were too deeply steeped in religious values and rituals. Not intending to make a fuss about it and with a mind to adjust herself in the new family, she started following all religious dictates.

Then came the day of Karva Chauth on which a married Hindu woman is expected to fast from morning till late in the night without even a sip of water for the well-being of her husband. Veena told her mother-in-law that she would not fast as her sugar level could drop and lead to complications.

But the old woman would have none of it. Veena was forced to keep fast and follow the strict regimen. Towards late afternoon, she started sweating profusely. All her requests to eat something fell on deaf ears. Minutes later, she fainted. Luckily, her brother came to visit and when he saw his sister's condition, he forcibly took her to the hospital where she was treated for hypoglycaemia. Fortunately, she did not go into diabetic coma.

☆ ☆ ☆

It does perplex me to believe how a husband's life can be extended by keeping his wife hungry for one day in a year. The goal of religion is to free and emancipate the mind. But, in practice, it works on the concept of fear – **If you do not do this, God will punish you.** Let us pause and think.

One is reminded of the words of a famous saint, who said –

"If by standing in water one could be pious, then the fish are the most pious of all.

If one could please God by not eating meat, then the cows and goats are the favourites of the Supreme, as they eat only grass."

Nothing to fear except fear

Fears and phobias form a very important, formidable and seemingly insurmountable aspect of the conditioning of human mind. It could be fear of some person, fear of an animal or even fear of failure. Every fear has its root in some initial thought or event, something that gave birth to it. And that particular incident so conditions the mind that every time one thinks of a similar thing, fear grips the mind.

The famous writer Dale Carnegie once wrote about a short tempered woman, whom everyone used to fear. One day he needed to go to her. When he heard of others' experiences with her, initially he too felt afraid of approaching her. But he analysed the fear he had in his mind and decided to go. When he reached her house, he saw her tending to her garden. He started talking to her about gardening and complemented her for having such beautiful plants and flowers. The little praise won her heart and he was able to achieve the purpose for which he had gone. If he had allowed his mind to be conditioned by the experiences of others, he would never have achieved his goal. He did not fear his fear. He made an attempt and succeeded.

No end to our Conditioning

Conditioning of the mind is not restricted to just culture, tradition, social norms and fear. It can have varied aspects, each as delimiting as the other. One may just be lacking in confidence because of conditioning thoughts. For example, "I am unlucky, I am a failure, I have no future, I cannot do this."

Let us try to analyse the self-degrading type of conditioning, which makes one feel useless and worthless in one's own eyes. The most embittered in this category are those who have tried again and again but have met repeated failures in life.

Actually, success and failure are but a part of life and they do not always reflect on one's capabilities or skills or intelligence.

Take the example of Abraham Lincoln. Everyone knows that he is considered as one of the greatest leaders of all times in the US but perhaps very few know that he had to taste failures in politics and elections many times before he was elected the President of the US in 1860. If he had taken his earlier failures to heart, he would never have reached such envious heights.

In reality, life never wants us to feel defeated by failures. Rather it wants us to take on further challenges with a dauntless spirit. In the Bhagvad Gita, Lord Krishna has said that you have the right over your actions, but not their fruits. One has to unlearn to negate thoughts like 'once a failure always a failure', 'once unlucky always unlucky' and keep on trying, for one knows not what promise life holds for us round the next corner.

> We cannot solve problems by using the same kind of thinking we used when we created them.
> – Abraham Lincoln

The following lines written by Buddha will help everyone to nurture self-awareness, go beyond beliefs, conditioning and get enlightened, which would lead to inner peace and happiness.

> *Do not believe what you have heard.*
> *Do not believe in traditions because it is handed down many generations.*
> *Do not believe in anything that has been spoken of many times.*
> *Do not believe because the written statements come from some old sage.*
> *Do not believe in conjecture.*
> *Do not believe in authority or teachers or elders.*
>
> *But after careful observation and analysis, when it agrees with reason and it will benefit one and all, then accept it and live by it.*

[Chapter Three]

God Makes You. You Make Your Attitude

Attitude is a little thing that makes a big difference.
– *Sir Winston Churchill*

Life is a shipwreck but we must not forget to sing in the lifeboats.

– *Voltaire*

You are your attitude. The way you perceive life and what it has to offer, makes you who you are. Life is an attitude and it is the only thing that matters for survival.

☆ ☆ ☆

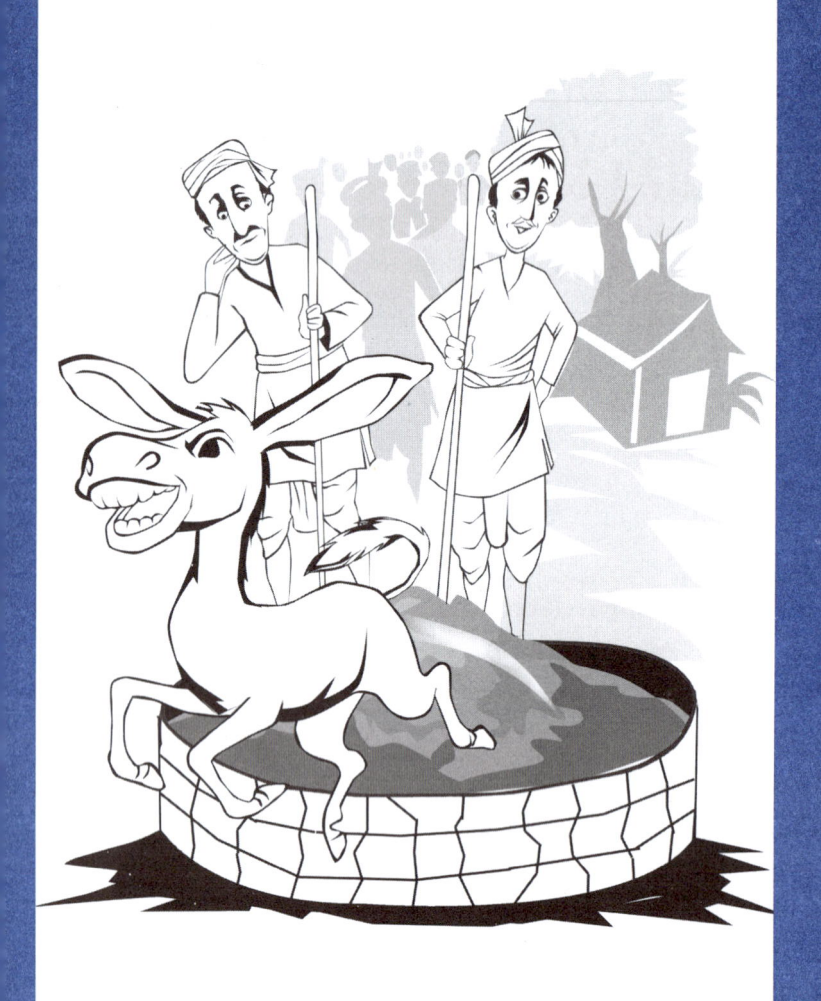

A farmer's donkey once fell into a deep dry well. The loud braying of the beast made the farmer rush to the spot. He tried to figure out a way to get it out. By then, his sons and some villagers had gathered around the well.

"The well is very deep," said the farmer.

"And the walls are caving in. So it is not even safe for anyone to climb down," said another.

"It will need too much of effort to get it out," was the opinion of yet another.

After a lot of discussion, the farmer decided to give it up. The well was too deep and it was a tough task. Moreover, the donkey was very old.

"It is not worth putting in so much of effort for this old beast. Let us bury it here itself," declared the farmer. Saying so, he got a few shovels and the men got to work. All around the well, there were mounds of loose earth. They started shoveling it into the well.

Some moments later, when they looked into the well, they were in for a surprise. The donkey was standing on top of the earth they had shoveled in and not buried under it. They shoveled some more earth to see what was happening. They realised that when the earth fell on the donkey, it shook it off. Because of the shoveling, the bottom of the well was moving up and the donkey was coming closer to the surface. The men started shoveling with added enthusiasm. Soon the whole well was filled with earth and the donkey jumped on to the hard ground. It was quite well and unhurt.

The farmer laughed aloud and said, "Here is a wonderful lesson for us. Life sure shovels dirt on one. But the trick is in shaking it off and moving a step up."

☆ ☆ ☆

The quitter gets nothing. The one who keeps striving ultimately wins. Just the act of trying is a big triumph! The difference between a quitter and winner is in their attitude. A problem can be a hurdle or a stepping stone towards success. It is up to us how we see it, whether we want to be a positive or negative person. Ultimately, it is this choice which has impact on everything in life – our work, our relationships and the kind of person we become. With positive thinking, life becomes happier, looks and feels better. And happiness makes us stronger. Negative thinking damages our spirit and affects us physically and mentally.

The world is full of struggles. To live is to struggle. Undoubtedly, we evolve and grow through struggle. A little change in attitude and victory over our mind

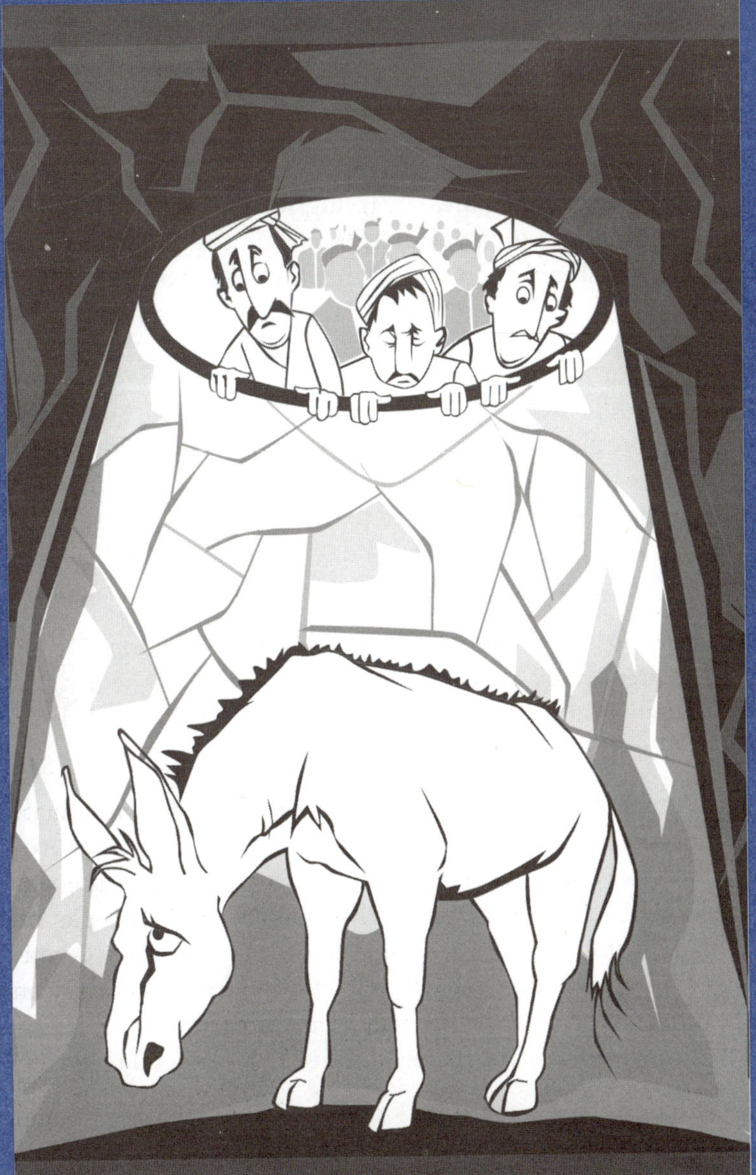

develops positivity, increases will power and confidence, leading to happiness.

Therefore, trying always, trying in spite of the problems, trying till one's last breath, trying till the very last ray of hope is shining and this is what life is all about.

Don't Close Your Book Too Soon

The initial debacles in life do frustrate all of us. Many of us are simply not willing to go on or try further. Frustration is one big reason why people remain unhappy in life. They become so devoid of hope that they are not even ready to see what the next moment or day has in store for them. They forget success might be waiting just round the corner.

Among my favourite authors is Sidney Sheldon. He has written many bestseller novels. But of all his works, the one that impressed me most was his biography titled *'The Other Side Of Me'*.

An incident from his early life stands out as a very good example for those who think they have lost all hope. Sidney was seventeen and worked in a drugstore as a delivery boy. He aspired to be an author, a novelist. But his parents could not afford to send him to college or get him proper education. Moreover, it was the time of great depression in the US and their family was living almost hand to mouth. Frustrated by it all, Sidney decided to put an end to his life.

One Saturday, when he knew no one would be at home, he stole sleeping pills from the drugstore and returned

God Makes You. You Make Your Attitude ■ 47

home. He was seated on his bed, about to gulp down the pills, when in walked his father. He had forgotten to take something and had come back home. He was left aghast when he realised what his son was about to do. When he questioned his son, Sidney said it was his life and he could do anything with it. His father saw a determined look on his face and asked him to just postpone what he was doing and take a walk with him.

For the next many minutes, his father talked to him as they walked along a road. He told him that life had so many beautiful things to offer. But he saw that his words were going unheeded by his son, who kept silent all along. Suddenly, his father remembered something and said, "I think you told me once you wanted to be a writer. Why not do that?"

Sidney replied that there was no hope for him, at which his father said, "This is not right. You do not know what could happen next day. Life is like a novel….You have no idea what is going to happen until you turn the page."

These words hit the mark. Something clicked in Sidney's mind. His father's words touched him deep and he thought, "He has a point. Every tomorrow is like the next page of a novel."

Seeing that his son was turning around, his father said, "I'd hate to see you close the book too soon…"

Sidney was saved by these words that day. He decided to proactively take charge of his life and mindfully decided

> We cannot direct the winds, but we can adjust the sails.
> – *Pavan Choudary*

> Most people give up just when they're about to achieve success. They quit on the one yard line. They give up at the last minute of the game, one foot from a winning touchdown.
> – *Ross Perot*

> I had the blues because I had no shoes until upon the street, I met a happy man who had no feet.
> – *A Persian Saying*

what he wanted to achieve. He did everything to achieve his goal thereafter. He became the master instead of a victim. His determination – his plan – change of attitude – his bravely wading through all the problems – were all his actions, his powers, within HIM and thus, he went on to become one of the greatest novelists of modern times.

Happiness is an attitude towards life. Socrates lived out this truth by personal example. He used to go barefoot. His philosophy of life was that happiness always comes from within; external factors can never give happiness.

One day when Socrates was looking keenly at the decorative articles in the market, one of his critics saw him and asked him somewhat smugly, "I thought these things did not make you happy."

Undisturbed by his intended barb, Socrates replied, "Actually I was observing that there are so many things in this world, without which I can live happily all along and remain contended as well."

"Diogenes was content with his bathtub, while Alexander was not happy even after conquering the world."

It is not the setbacks or the problems that make us unhappy. It is our attitude towards them. I strongly believe things are never as bad as they may appear. We should not look at things as they are, let us look at how they can be.

Life is all about choices. We choose how to react, how to behave. It is entirely our choice. The only thing that is truly ours and that no one can take from us is our ATTITUDE.

Begin to change your attitude, and your vision of the world will change.

Everything will be peaceful & good. This is the highest knowledge – Vedantic Vision

Choose your attitude wisely. It is who you are.

[Chapter Four]

Never give up

"Most of the important things in the world have been accomplished by people who have kept on trying when there seemed to be no hope at all."

– *Dale Carnegie*

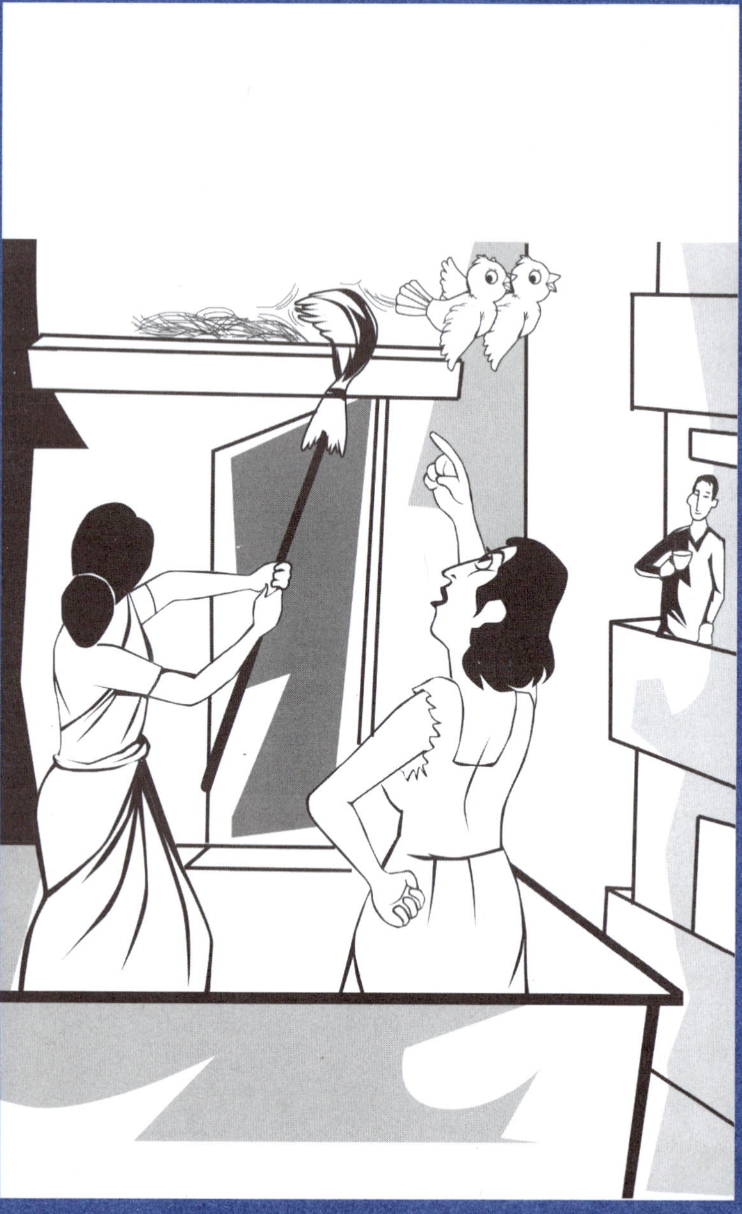

It was a beautiful spring morning a few years ago when I stepped on to my balcony with a cup of tea in my hand. As I sipped the brew, the peace of the morning was suddenly shattered by the shrill chirping of some birds. I turned in that direction and saw two sparrows wildly flying around another balcony. My happy heart sank as I saw the reason for their agitation. In the balcony, stood a maid with a long broom, with her mistress by her side, loudly giving instructions.

"Get it all out!" she cried.

The broom brushed over a ledge above the balcony door and down came crashing a mass of straws, dry grass and leaves. The birds had just lost their newly built nest!

An hour later, I happened to look out of the window and was surprised by what I saw. The birds were at it again, bringing straw and grass and rebuilding their nest at the very same place!

Over the next few weeks, it became a daily ritual. The maid would sweep away the bundle of straw and next morning,

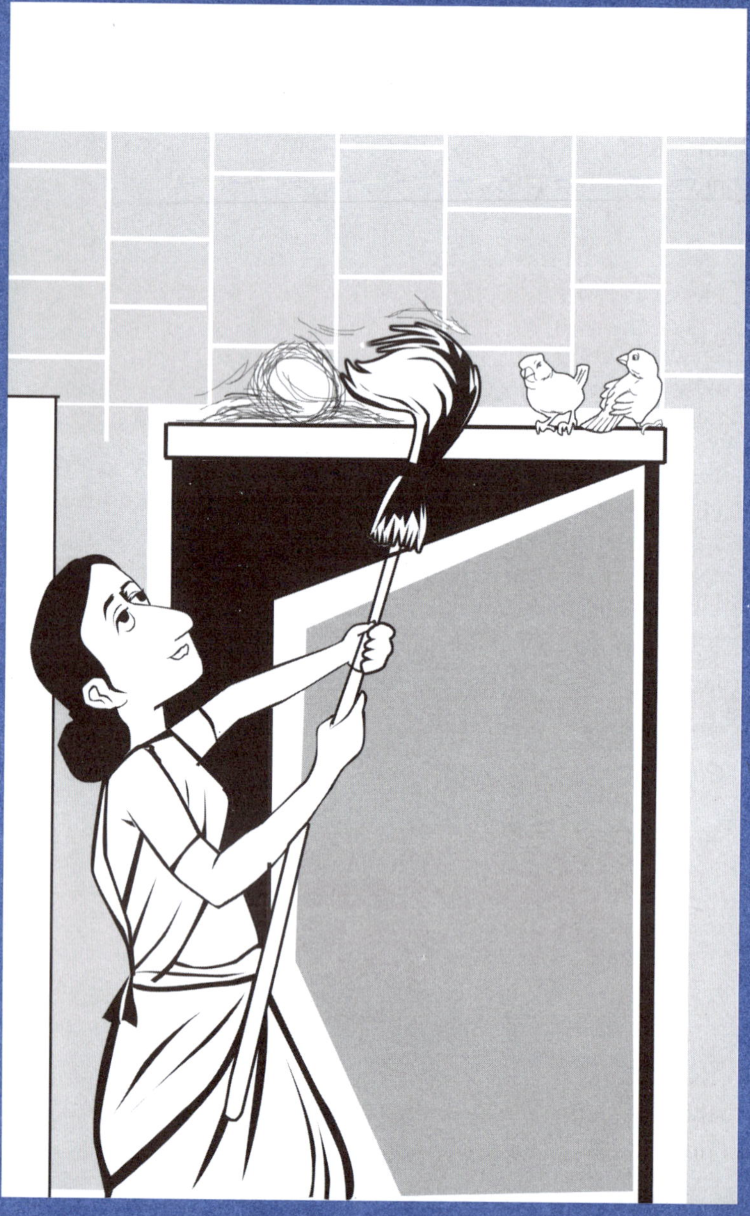

it would be there again! She did not seem to tire of the task and neither did the birds. They seemed to be born with a never-say-die spirit!

It set me thinking.

How often do set-backs propel our inner engines?

What do we do when we suffer a set back? What we do when disaster strikes? Do we have the courage to start all over again? Or, we get disheartened and leave it.

How often we hear people say, "That's enough." "The effort is just not worth it!" "I am tired of it all." "It's all too much."

Don't we easily give up, sit and curse fate or circumstances for our failures?

The two untiring birds epitomize patience and the spirit of never giving up. They just continue to chirp, sing and go on with their work, patiently building and rebuilding, till their nest is ready again; and never giving up. They instill into a person the ability to move forward and ultimately emerge successful.

Are you being fooled by your circumstances?

More often than not, we give up efforts during the course of a struggle because our circumstances appear so overwhelming. The mind gets fooled into thinking that there is no way out and trying would just be a waste of time and resources.

The mind accepts only what is logical. It gathers data from what is going on around and then comes to a conclusion. In itself, the mind is not capable of seeing beyond logic. It is very much limited in its perception by what it perceives in the present. And so it can get fooled. Fooled, because no one really knows what could happen tomorrow or even the next moment.

You might be ready to abandon your efforts because circumstances do not favour you. But what if things improve in the future?

Your mind might say that there is no way that you can win and you in turn, may prepare yourself to give up the struggle. But what if there is another way out which is not obvious to you today but could become clear sometime later?

> Never let your head hang down. Never give up and sit down to grieve. Find another way.
>
> –Satchel Paige *(The American baseball legend)*

There is bound to be some way! Only the mind may not perceive it at that point in time. The mind is a tool of rational thinking but not always is it reliable. If you find it hard to believe then just think – how come a tortoise entered into a race with a hare…and won! Fine, one might say that it is just a fable! But it is a fable with a powerful message. It not only conveys that 'slow and steady wins the race', it brings through the idea that our mind can be easily fooled.

So, if your mind tells you that you are in a no-win situation, then learn to say shut-up to it once in a while, for there are thousands of real life incidents that tell us how people came out as winners, even in situations where the mind told them that they could never succeed.

When Henry Ford put forward his idea to manufacture a motor car for the masses, none other than the great scientist Thomas Alva Edison told him to give up his idea as he believed it to be worthless. But Ford did not abandon his dream and went on to establish a company that manufactured cars for the masses!

The never-give-up spirit also came in handy for the great 19th century Italian violin player Niccolo Paganini. Once when he was giving a performance, a string of his violin snapped. But without even a pause, he continued to play. Just a few seconds later, another string snapped, and then a third. Just one string remained on the violin, but so well did he improvise that the audience were left spellbound by his mastery. Where another violinist might have apologized and stopped, he went on, and that particular performance of his is rated amongst his best.

The incident if anything tells us that hurdles are bound to appear in life, but do not let the mind be 'fooled' into believing that one cannot proceed any further. Do not give up, come what may and you will surely find a way to win! But if you think, you have lost it then you will lose.

If you think you are beaten, you are.
If you think you dare not, you don't.
If you'd like to win but think you can't,
It's almost a cinch you won't . . .

– *Walter D. Wintle*

Success might just be round the corner

Many of us give up at the last minute, when just another step could take us to victory, to the trophy, to the goal! It could be because of two reasons – discouragement from others or self defeat/ lack or exhaustion of self-motivation. In every such situation, although difficult, one should try to remember that whether it was flying in the air or diving deep into the ocean or even setting foot on the moon; all has been achieved through man's determination to succeed even after repeated failures.

You might have heard that every failure is a step in the direction of your goal. But how? Encountering failure is an elimination process. It is through failure alone that you can eliminate a wrong way of doing a thing until you find the right way.

The devilish forces in life are determined to strike us down at times. But it is just to test our strength. If in trying times one gets impatient, it only breeds fear, stress, disillusionment and unhappiness. It is patience and patience alone, before which difficulties and obstacles disappear and you can then conquer destiny.

So, get rid of impatience, persevere harder in times of pressure and just when it seems like it is the end. Persevere with patience and calmness of the mind. At the same time, visualise success and think how great it would be to get there.

> How poor are they that have not patience;
> What wound did ever heal but by degree?
> – *Shakespeare*

The key is to always push yourself, keep chugging with single minded focus, no matter what happens. Even if you lose once, build more momentum. Strive to be stronger. Do not shrink back. It is persistence and persistence alone, which will win the day. Wherever you are headed, you will definitely reach there if you just keep going, patiently.

> Remember:
>
> *"A concentrated mind succeeds not only because it can solve problems with greater dispatch, but also because problems have a way of somehow vanishing before it's focused energies, without even requiring to be solved."* – Swami Kriyananda

[Chapter Five]

This too Shall Pass

> *'The difficulties of life are intended to make us better, not bitter.'*

This simple line in Hebrew holds the truth about life – 'This too shall pass'. A truth that is eternal and that is the key to true and lasting peace!

The source of this inspiring phrase is the story of the famous Jewish king – Solomon. Solomon thought of teaching one of his ministers, Benaiah, a lesson. He assigned him an almost impossible task to find a ring so magical that, upon wearing it, ones mood would swing from unhappiness to happiness and vice versa. The time given to him was six months. Both Solomon and Benaiah knew that there was no such ring. But just before the end date, Benaiah decided to visit one of the poorest places in Jerusalem. He thought of taking a chance and asked one of the merchants if he had such a ring. The poor but wise merchant picked a ring and etched the words "_Gam zeh ya'avor_" – This too shall pass, and handed it over to Benaiah. When Benaiah read the inscription, he smiled and ran with his find to King Solomon. The king was both overjoyed and contemplative as the deep wisdom behind those words touched him like a silent realization – Joys in life are ephemeral. They don't last and soon the clouds of sadness overshadow them. Similarly, sorrows are also not permanent. With time, the brightness of joy dispels them. This simple wisdom brought immense peace to the

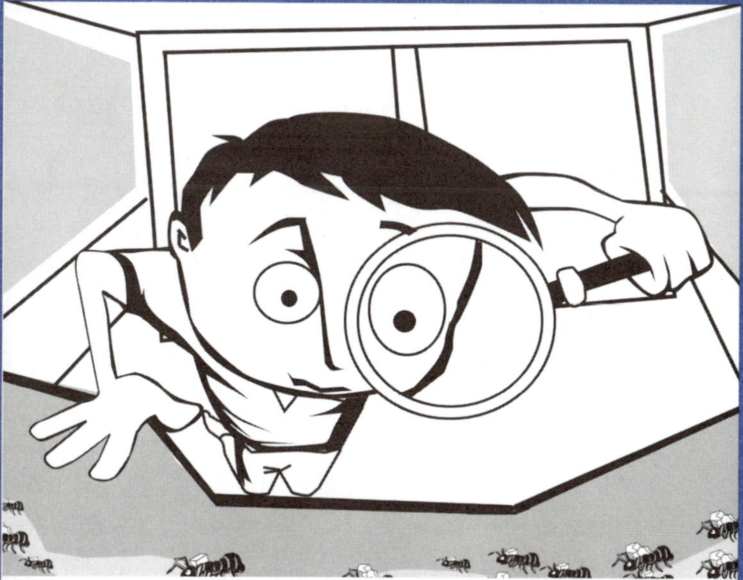
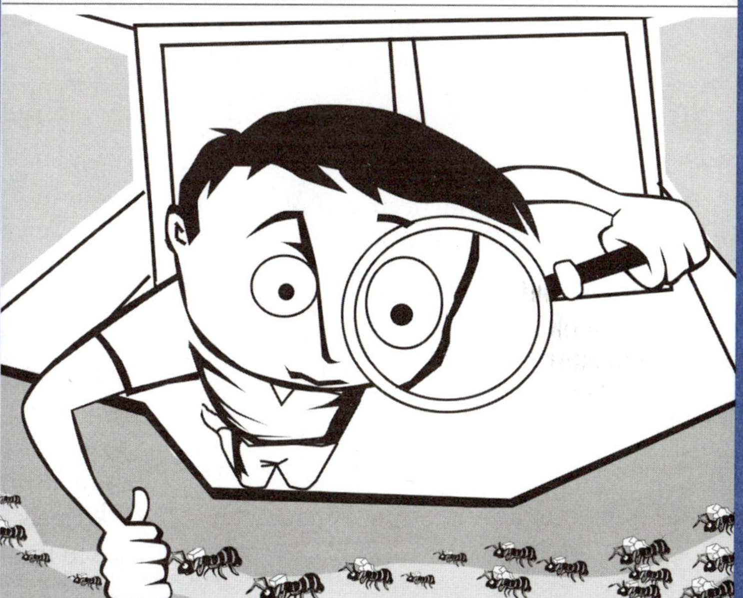

disturbed and turbulent heart of the king. Never again did he despair in life.

We mostly oscillate between joys and sorrows of life. Joys make us happy and feel on top of the world, while sorrows put us under a dark cloud. The truth is that life is like an everlasting game of light and shadow. One moment, the sun shines through brightly, and the next moment, dark clouds obscure the light. Everything is short lived. To realize this, is the greatest lesson that life aspires to teach us. That is, to show equanimity in every moment of life and to remain peaceful and contented in every joy or sorrow, knowing that it shall also pass!

Also, if fate has overshadowed one's life with gloom, then it is always wise to remember what Winston Churchill once said, 'If you're going through hell, keep going.'

There is an interesting analogy to This too Shall Pass in The Ant Philosophy.

Ants have an amazing four part philosophy:
The first is, **Ants never quit**.
That's a good philosophy.
If they're heading somewhere and you try to stop them;
They'll look for another way.
They'll climb over,
They'll climb under,
They'll climb around.

Keep looking around for another way – to get where you want to reach.

The second part is, **Ants think winter all summer.**
That's an important perspective.
You can't be so naïve to think that summer will last forever.
So ants gather in their winter food in the middle of summer.
It is important to think about tough times and struggles.
Struggles which may have to be encountered in the future and be prepared for them.
As the good old military saying goes:
The more you sweat in peace, the less you bleed at war.
So, think ahead and plan.

The third part of the ant philosophy is **Ants think summer all winter.**
It is so important to look for the 'light at the end of the tunnel'.
Think positive so that you could gather strength.
During winter, ants remind themselves,
"This won't last long; we'll soon be out of here."
And on the first warm day, the ants are out.
If it turns cold again, they'll dive back down,
But then they come out the first warm day.
They can't wait to get out.
So even when we are tied up in trouble,
Always look for opportunities and get out in the first place itself.
May not be successful but it is worth a try.

And here is the last part of the ant's philosophy.
How much will an ant gather during the summer to prepare for the winter?
"All that he possibly can."
What an incredible philosophy–
The 'all-that-you-possibly-can' philosophy.
Put in the best effort when you can;
There may be a time ahead when you cannot.
Extract the maximum when you have an opportunity;
Because you may not get another opportunity.

[Chapter Six]

Mind Over Matter

Men are not prisoners of fate, but prisoners of their own minds.

– *Franklin D. Roosevelt*

Logicians have but ill-defined
  as rational as the human mind.
    Logic, they say, belongs to man,
      But let them prove it if they can.

– *Oliver Goldsmith*

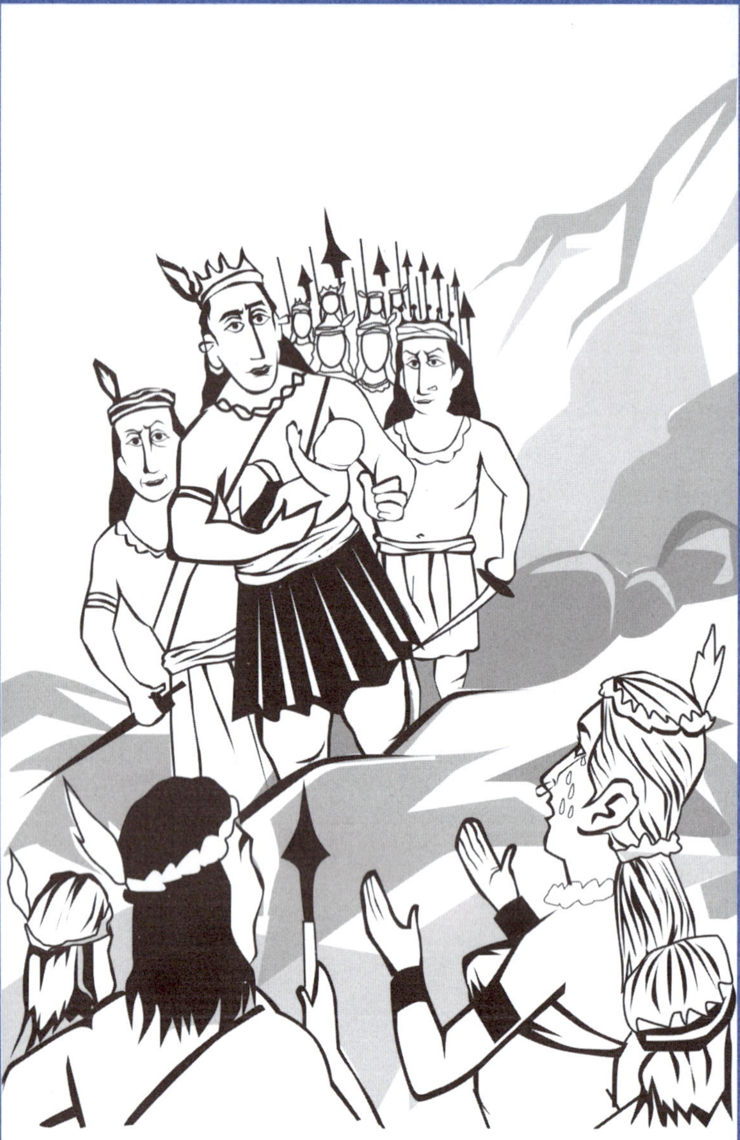

Many years ago, there lived two warring tribes, one on the plains and the other on hills. They were constantly at war with each other for several generations. The tribe living on the hills was more aggressive of the two and often attacked the tribe on the plain. With time, the people of the plains mastered the art of defense and left all the attacks futile. For some time, there was a lull. Then all of a sudden one night, the hill people launched a surprise attack on the plain dwellers and along with the other loot carried away an infant boy.

For the first time, a strong team of young men took off to climb the hills in an attempt to retrieve the child. They knew that the hill tribe lived across six hills and it would be a long and arduous journey for them, as never had any person from the plain climbed the hills earlier. They crossed two hills with great difficulty in the first five days. As the third hill loomed before them, they were filled with dismay. The hill slope was almost vertical and appeared insurmountable at many places. They had a long discussion amongst themselves and at last decided to give up.

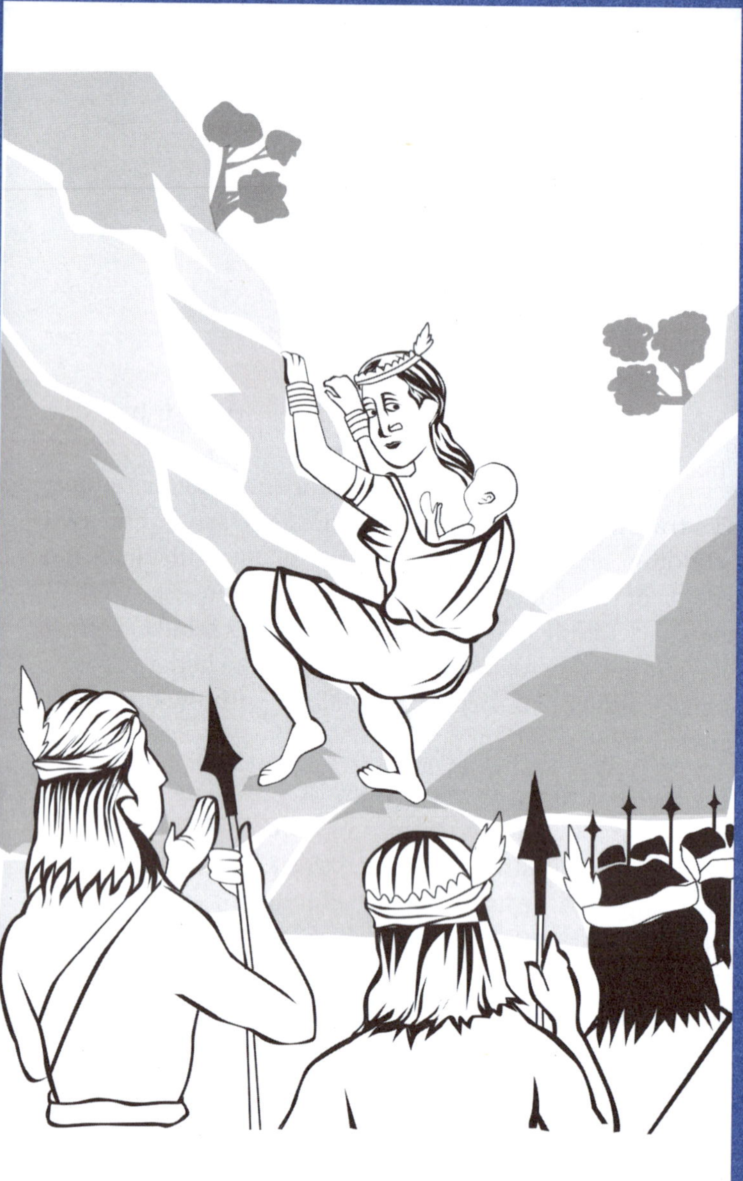

Just then, one of them shouted, "Look up there! Someone is climbing down."

Sure, there was someone up there, carefully climbing down with a load tied to her back. At first, they were astounded to find out that it was a woman! Secondly, they were in for a greater shock when they saw the lady at the foot of the hill. She stood with the infant boy safely tucked at her back, the same child they had just given up to rescue.

The bewildered leader of the team asked, 'How did you manage to climb the six hills so fast and rescue the child?'

The woman looked at him and said, 'Because this is my child!'

☆ ☆ ☆

Make your choice:

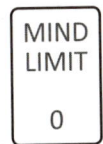

MIND LIMIT	MIND LIMIT
0	∞

The story speaks about the infinite power of the mind, highlighting the triumph of a strong determined mind over a weak and wavering mind. Mind actually has no limits – neither at the bottom nor at the top! It can be made to climb any heights of achievement. At the same time, if not mastered, it can be made to plunge into any depths of dismal failure and frustration. You possess the power of choice. Choose it rightly. The choice is yours.

My mind, my kingdom

There is no limit to the powers of this kingdom of ours. Tell yourself, I am the king of my mind. I am the ruler of this inner domain. Only then will you recognize and enjoy the infinite powers of this mind. You have been authorized to manage this kingdom, manage it in a positive manner. If our choice is correct, the mind can give us everlasting peace and happiness for a lifetime. Remember:

We are what we think we are!

The state of your mind determines what sort of life experiences you have. Whether it is getting a degree, earning a living, marriage, parenting, old-age; life can be rich and full of experiences to share or it can become a chronology of your existence on this planet.

We are the creators of our own "Heaven" and "Hell."

> *Lord Krishna says:*
> *"One must deliver himself with the help of his mind and not degrade himself.*
> *The mind is the friend of the conditioned soul, and his enemy as well."* (Bhagwad Gita, Chapter 6-5.6)

Mind is the cause of bondage and also the cause of liberation. It is stressed here that the mind must be so trained that it can deliver from the mire of conscience.

> *"For him, who has conquered the mind, the mind is his best friend;*
> *but for one who has failed to do so, his mind will remain his greatest enemy."*

One who cannot control his mind always lives with the greatest enemy and thus his life is spoiled. But when the mind is conquered, one abides by the dictates of the Personality of the God head, who is residing within everyone.

Consider this: We allow petty things to affect our peace of mind. And when 'we allow', we become disturbed.

☆ ☆ ☆

A village priest was jealous of Lord Buddha's fame. He happened to meet Buddha on the road while the latter was passing through the village. The priest started hurling abuses at Buddha. But the great master kept walking unperturbed. When he had walked out of the village, Buddha's disciple angrily asked, 'Why did you not reply to his abuses?'

Buddha smiled and said, 'Which abuses? He did try to give me some but I did not take any!'

☆ ☆ ☆

The pursuit of More ... & More ... & More

'Some have too much, yet still do crave;
I little have, and seek no more.
They are but poor, though much they have.
And I am rich with little store.
They poor, I rich; they beg, I give;
They lack, I leave; they pine, I live.'
– *Sir Edward Dyer*

We don't have to blame any outsider for our lust, cravings and addictions. The need to acquire more than what we require is not imposed on us from outside. It is self-imposed. A swanky car, a lavish villa and even immense fame may not keep you happy. A mind achieves happiness only through mastering one's thoughts. Even if people are bent upon disturbing your peace, you can be calm within, depending upon, how you choose to use your mind. Fulfillment and happiness is always available to you. Exercise the correct option. It is not easy, but certainly achievable.

Are you a Mind-Slave ?

I was in fourth class when I got into the habit of postponing things for a later time. If there was homework to be done, my mind would say, "You can always do it later." And that "later" never came, as a result of which my grades suffered. My father clarified, "Tomorrow never comes. Always remember that. The mind will play tricks and make you think there is a lot of time. But you must understand that if something is to be done, it should be done instantly. Otherwise, the mind will never allow you to get down to the task."

Fortunately, I was at an age where my mind was not conditioned and could be easily molded. My father's advice did help me overcome my mind's game plan. Whenever it tried to lead me astray, I would refuse to listen to it and slowly I learnt to ignore its bickering.

Many people in order to get instant happiness, continue to remain in conflict and find it hard to battle its inescapable trap.

☆ ☆ ☆

My classmate at school, Vinesh was a very bright student and an excellent sportsman. After school, he fell into bad company and took to drugs. His addiction made him steal and that is when his family admitted him to a drug de-addiction centre! That was the last I saw him for a long time.

Years later, I met another old schoolmate of mine, Pankaj. He was with a frail man, who looked somewhat familiar. I was aghast to recognize Vinesh! His physical built quite an envy of all was reduced to a mere caricature and his cheerful, robust self to a dismal disbelief! Vinesh confessed how he was tortured at the de-addiction centre. Law does not permit physical torture but he was not spared whenever he demanded drugs. His urge coupled with stealing habits got the worse of him. He was thrashed with sticks. But somehow the centre changed his habits and got him off drugs.

Vinesh needed a job and I knew of an opening just suitable for him. We did not meet for some months until I ran into him again and discovered that he was on a "high" once again.

"Vinesh, have you forgotten the mental and physical torture you went through that you have started all over again?" I panicked and asked.

"Don't worry," he grinned. "I am now under perfect control. I take only a little bit. I won't let it enslave me once more."

"But isn't that how you started by taking only a bit. And you got trapped."

"Not this time! I have not forgotten what happened to me at the de-addiction centre. I will never go beyond a limit."

When he had left, I stood wondering at the fickleness of the human mind. What traps it lays! What convincing arguments it gives! When I saw Vinesh next, he was worse off than ever before and it set me thinking! Is the mind really one's best friend? Should one listen to it all the time? Why not treat it like your own child and not spoil it with excessive pampering. Constant vigil is required to stop the mind from going berserk.

> Be master of the mind rather than be mastered by the mind. –Zen

☆ ☆ ☆

Smoking, obesity, alcoholism is persisting because we welcome the sermon – "do it tomorrow". Our resolutions cow down before the voice of our mind. Fighting weight problems become herculean – You can fast and exercise for days but within a week you can resume to uncontrolled eating. Counseling, joining a gym – nothing seems to help. Advise from family and friends can bring about temporary change, but often one would succumb to the mind's craving for more and more food.

Our psyche at times becomes our foe. It encourages wrong habits, which become hard to give up. Ever faked illness to enjoy a movie? Ever bribed the traffic policeman to get away from a heavy challan? We tend to choose the convenience option suggested by our intellect.

The mind actually behaves like a restless child who has set his heart upon something and wants it immediately. No amount of cajoling can make it see a reason. It wants instant gratification unmindful of the consequences. Instant happiness is the nature of the mind. It does not believe in postponement of pleasure, as the child does not know when to stop wanting, so does the intellect! Or just how much is enough! Your conscience might stop you from having another drink, but the mind is willing to raise another toast for you.

> My heart tells me to give up, but my mind won't let me
>
> – Anonymous.

Mindful – Mindless nature of the mind

God has given us the mind. It is one of the greatest miracles of Nature. There is nothing as powerful and as wonderful in this world as the mind. And with the mind comes two great things. One is the power to think, and the second is the capacity to store those thoughts. Our mind is like a computer that can analyse and store facts. But it depends on the person operating the computer, what he wants to analyse and what he wants to store.

Our mind never stops or pauses even for a moment. One thought after another keeps passing by unconsciously. It enjoys working overtime.

Consider this: One is reading the newspaper. A robbery has taken place. The news impacts the mind and it conjures up fleeting images of theft in his house, fights with the robbers, untoward happening with the family members and so on and so forth. Even before you finish reading the whole news, your mind saps itself of all tranquility!

On a different note, an advertisement of a luxury apartment can set your mind racing. The need to change the house, selecting new furniture, designing its comfort level and planning its EMIs has happened even before there is a house.

This is what the mind does best – weave dreams! Just sow a tiny seed and soon you will have hundreds of looming thoughts crowding your mind.

The mind keeps creating situations and keeps providing solutions. Often, the situations are unreal and so are the solutions. This continuous flow of thoughts cannot be stopped. At least not willfully!

Handling thoughts

Our mind is like a flowing river. Dams on rivers survive because water is allowed to flow through, in a regulated manner, from time to time. If a dam is built over

> The human condition; lost in thought.
> – *Eckhart Tolle*

a river and there is no leeway, it can burst because of the pressure of the accumulated water. Similarly, if anyone tries to stop the flow of thoughts, it will simply destroy the brain!

It is impossible to stop the chain of thoughts but possible to redirect them. You can choose to think either positively or negatively to affect the mind in a controlled or an uncontrolled way. The outcome will be either happiness galore or sorrow in plenty.

> One who controls the mind attains supreme peace in life.
> – *Lord Krishna*

Attitude is an offshoot of mind. If one has a 'happy go lucky' attitude, then all negative aspects of life get buffered and vice-versa. We might not be able to change the circumstances or the people in our lives but our approach/attitude towards them can be altered.

Tuning the mind

'Everything is based on mind, is led by mind, is fashioned by mind. If you speak and act with a polluted mind, suffering will follow, as the wheels of an oxcart follow the footsteps of the ox.
Everything is based on mind, is led by mind, is fashioned by mind. If you speak and act with a pure mind, happiness will follow, as a shadow clings to a form.

Life in its protean states that of stress, strain, tension, obstacles, setbacks, frustrations and failures pose a

challenge. In such a scenario,
How can one revel in a state of everlasting joy?
How can one achieve calmness in the existing chaos of the world?
How can it be done?
Answer: Meditation.

What is MEDITATION?

I am the Chairman. I am the Director. I am the Father. I am the Husband. I am the Boss. I am the wife. I am so—and—so.

> Learn to be silent. Let your quiet mind listen and absorb.
> – *Pythagoras*

Let's pause for a while. Think what all this means. Are we defining ourselves or our functions? These are the roles, I play. In reality, this is not me; this is not 'I'. Then, the question arises if this is not 'I', what is 'I'?

I am something for sure. I am at some place within, which I can't see. All my roles and thoughts are stored therein – a storehouse within me. It is like a treasury, where infinite riches are lying. This place is invisible and silent. To extract anything from there, all we have to do is to open our mental eyes (through meditation). Meditation helps us to access this storehouse and discover that treasure. Meditation allows us to still the mind. The path of meditation leads us to use the mind correctly. It does not force the mind to be quiet, instead it finds the quiet that is already there.

> In the presence of a silent mind the dance of joy is experienced.
> – *Anonymous*

How does Meditation help?

The deluge of thoughts leaves one overwhelmed. Thoughts go on ceaselessly in our mind. It is estimated that on an average, an individual has about fifty thousand thoughts every day. But the real problem is that the same thoughts are repeated the next day. Therefore, what we had yesterday, we are having today and we will have tomorrow as well. Our mind is filled with the same chatter. We are so caught up in this daily routine that we pay no conscious attention to them.

Meditation acquaints you with any excess baggage that you may be carrying in your mind in the form of past hurts, anger, frustration, jealousy and other negative feelings. Meditation helps in reducing the number of thoughts. At the same time, it enables us to enter in between the spaces of thoughts. And when this happens, the mind perches quietly, becomes calm, peaceful and flowers from within.

It was through meditation alone that Narendra, an ordinary boy of Bengal, came to be known as Swami Vivekananda. Through self-help and self education He wrote:

> *Deep, deep within is the soul, the Essential Man, the Atman.*
> *Turn the mind inward and become united to that, and from that*
> *Stand point of stability, the gyrations of mind can be watched and*
> *facts observed, which are to be found in all persons.*
> *Such facts, such data are to be found by those who go deep enough.*

Make meditation an integral part of living. Let us learn to be silent, quieten our minds and become our friends.

Meditation is not Concentration

It is generally misconceived that meditation and concentration are one and the same thing. They are totally different. Concentration is focusing your mind to achieve a task; to do. It is a mental exercise – with focus on the object of attention. Concentration calls for analysis, judgment, condemnation, controlling of thoughts and choosing. Meditation is seeing the mind as a witness to our thoughts. We simply observe thoughts. We are just a witness. We visualize them without any analysis, without suppression or without any concentration. Here, we are a non-doer. Therefore, it is effortless. This is our true and original nature by birth.

How to Cultivate a quiet mind? How does one meditate?

> *Pascal, a French philosopher wrote in 17th century, "All men's miseries derive from not being able to sit quietly in a room alone."*

There are many techniques. Basically, sit in a quiet place, observe your breath and later, your thoughts. Do not make any attempt to stop them. It is like the flow of water. Any attempt to stop the flow will bounce back and strike with greater force. Just be vigilant. Also be patient. In a few days time, you will see the gaps between thoughts as silence. It is in silence alone that communication starts.

Just as an 'agitated mind' disturbs and saddens us, so a 'stilled mind' calms and pleases us. In simple words, the same mind that makes us weak and vulnerable when left uncontrolled can be a source of immense strength and energy when properly controlled.

What role does Chanting play?

While learning to deal with mental chatter through meditation, a normal practice, chanting is a very effective way of calming the mind. Chanting is a very useful adjunct to various meditation practices. When you give yourself to chanting, you are engaged and freeing up the vital energy of the body-mind. Then you fill your hearts with loving vibrations of sound. Use chanting to transform your moods; and "don't forget to enjoy the silence after chanting." My guru had said;

> *"Give yourself to the chant so that the chant chants you."*

Cerebral Food for thought

Some universal truths can also make the mind happy and joyful! Here are some such gems of eternal wisdom passed on down the ages.

- Determine to be happy: Happiness is your creation, only yours. The yearning to spend each minute in joy and not wallow in worries or troubles is the key to living a wholesome life. Imagine your mind to be a weighing balance keeping the troubles in line with the joys.

- No one has everything, but everyone has something: The greatest delusion we all live in is that material things bring us happiness whereas, it is things needed for the mind that fetch us peace. So don't fret about what you don't have. Rejoice about what you have! And even if you are robbed of all your possessions, no one can rob you of your happiness, the state of your mind, your own personal inner kingdom!

- Live in the present: Let bygones be bygones. Similarly, let the future be. Worrying about the future and dwelling on the past can change nothing.

- Do not react: If it is difficult then try postponing your reaction. The mind is conditioned to react instantly like our reflexes but we can nip this habit!

Abraham Lincoln, the President of USA always wrote a fitting reply to every letter that criticized him or accused him. He would later burn his response. This, he said made him feel better and at the same time avoided friction. Postponing reactions for a day or two makes us realize that it is useless to react.

- It is impossible to please everybody. No matter what you do, no matter how good your intentions, there will be someone out there with a different opinion. One should never worry about criticism.

'If criticism is unjustified then ignore it, if it is justified then learn from it.'

- Learn to be kind, compassionate and loving to others. When the mind shows compassion towards those who are suffering from pain and the wish to remove the miseries of others, the desire to do evil is eliminated. Happiness and love never run out no matter how much you share.

- Give and serve selflessly. Doing a bit can make a difference to the life of someone, somewhere. If you have the good fortune and the privilege of being able to give, then you in fact become a hand of God! Just feel that it is He giving through you and you will experience a bliss experienced never before.

> *Remember:*
> *A mind at peace, a mind centered and not focused on harming others, is stronger than any physical force in the universe.'*
> *— Wayne Dyer*

[Chapter Seven]

Focus Your Energy

"Concentrate all your thoughts upon the work at hand.
The sun's rays do not burn until brought to a focus."

— *Alexander Graham Bell*

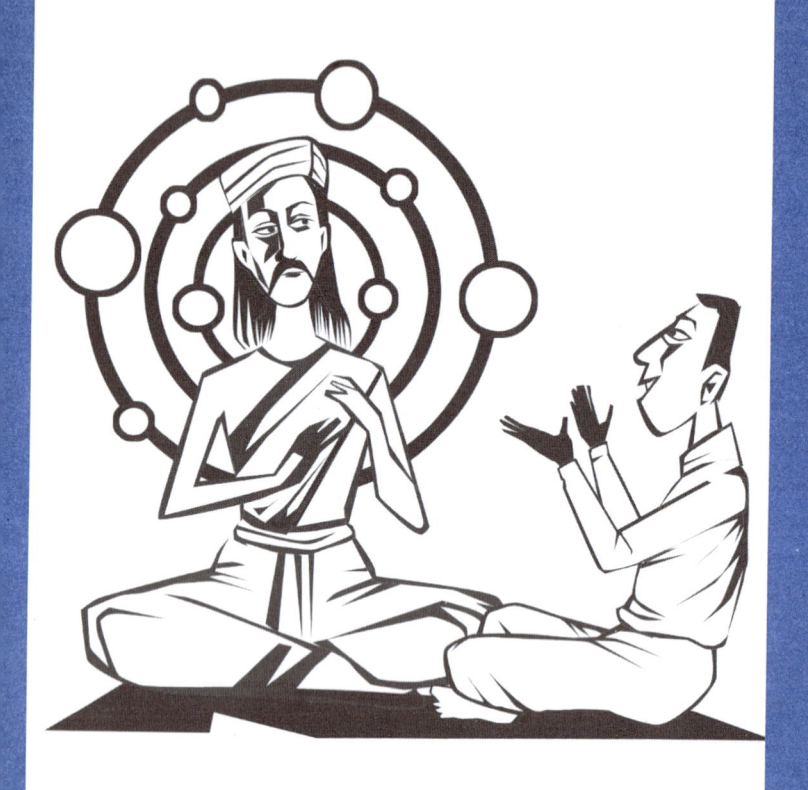

I was on a brief stay at the ashram of Swami Satyanand, my spiritual Guru. I observed him minutely, trying to understand his vision of life and the manner in which he saw the world. What I saw left me a bit perplexed. He seemed to spend his day in the most ordinary way. Then how was he different from us ordinary people? I wanted to find out.

One day, I gathered courage and approached him. "Swami ji, I want to ask you something."

He smiled and said, "Tell me, what is it?"

"I know you are an enlightened person, but… what do you do the whole day?"

"Well, I get up in the morning, I have a bath, pray, I eat, I work. I meet people. In the evening, I say my prayers, take dinner and go to bed," he replied.

"But that is nothing different from what we all do."

He seemed to understand my dilemma and said, "Well, when I bathe, I bathe. When I eat, I eat. When I work, I work."

I protested slightly, "But I also do all this. What is so different?"

He smiled at my exasperation and said, "You are missing the point. When you sleep, you dream. When you are awake, you are really sleeping because you live in the dream world of your thoughts. When you are having a bath, you think of the day ahead. When you eat, your mind is elsewhere. When you are at work, you think of home and when you are at home, you are worried about your work. In reality, your mind is always far away from where you are."

His words made me think deep.

He went on, "As a result, you remain divided and are not able to concentrate on what you are doing. When I do something, my entire focus is on that action and I do not think of anything else."

"But how does it matter if we are thinking of something else, while being engaged in some physical action? I would say it is a good use of time, doing two things at one time and that is better time management," I remarked.

"It matters a lot. In fact, it could make all the difference between success and failure. Thought is a great source of energy and inspiration. Focusing your thoughts means focusing your complete energy on an action. When this happens, the action becomes perfect and success gets ensured."

Next day, when I went for my morning walk I decided to concentrate fully on the process of walking – no chatting on the phone and no planning for work. I entered the park and focused all my thoughts on this activity. I mentally observed the muscles of my legs as I moved forward, and those of my hands as I swung them along. I focused on each creak the joints made. I became totally engrossed in the action of walking and very soon, I felt as if I was not walking but gliding smoothly with each muscle moving in perfect rhythm. I continued to do this for about a week and discovered a remarkable improvement in my state of health. I was also mentally more relaxed and at peace with myself.

I realised that I had turned the activity of walking into meditation. It was almost a revelation. I did feel that any piece of work can be made totally fulfilling by focusing. On the other hand, when the mind is allowed to wander in any direction, the focus is lost, resulting in avoidable anxiety and tension.

What if every day of our lives we were to do this? We cannot imagine the giant capacity we can immediately command, when we focus all our resources on mastering a single area of our lives.

Focus Vs The Monkey Mind

Buddhists refer to the human brain as the 'monkey mind' which keeps chattering ceaselessly. If this chattering could be stopped somehow, one would then attain the 'Buddha mind', wherein all the energy of the mind remains focused. And this ultimately is the key to success and happiness.

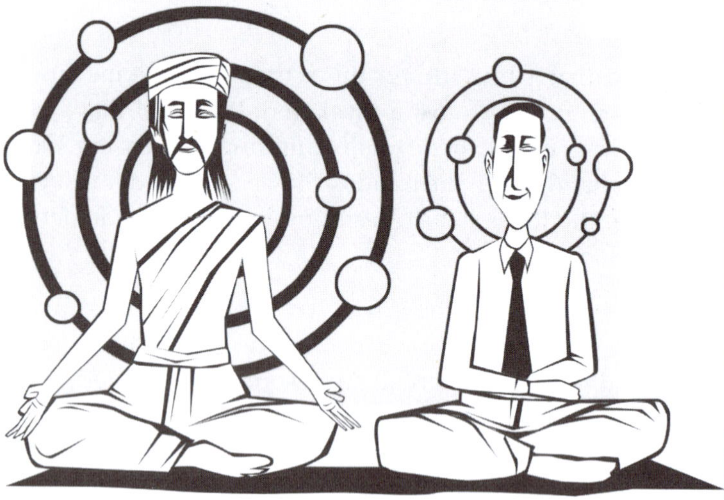

There is no doubt that mind is a source of infinite energy. We are very powerful because of the infinite capacity of the mind. But not all of us are aware of this power or what all it can achieve or how this power can be tapped. Mostly, thoughts of worrying, criticizing, jealousy, envy, greed, anger, passion and so on disperse and scatter this energy. In other words, these emotions are forms of energy. Therefore, anger is energy, jealousy is energy…and if one knew how to channelize this energy, one can achieve amazing levels of success and happiness. Whatever be the field of one's work, not just materially, in the spiritual pursuits too, success would be easier and faster to achieve.

☆ ☆ ☆

Once there was a young man who was well-trained in martial arts and was known to be the best archer in his country. One day he came to know that in the mountains lived a master who was even better. The youth decided to go and see, and if true, learn more from that master.

After a long journey and much searching, he found the master living in a cave. The youth approached him and said, "I am the best archer in this country. But I have come to know that you are even better. Can I see what you can do?"

The master smiled and said, "Let me see your skill first. There is that tree in the valley. You can see the dark spot on its trunk. Aim for it."

> It is wise to direct your anger towards problems – not people; to focus your energies on answers – not excuses.
> – *William Arthur Ward*

The youth raised his bow and put an arrow to it. Then he took aim and let the arrow fly. It struck the mark. He then turned to face the master.

The old master got up and said, "See if you can do this."

He then walked to the edge of a precipice, stood on one leg and without any wavering he shot an arrow that flew and sank into the tail of the arrow the youth had shot.

The youth walked uncertainly to the edge of the precipice and as he looked down, his feet started to shake. There was no question of standing on just one foot at the edge. Nevertheless, he tried but found himself shaking and trembling. He tried to raise his bow, but there was no chance of his finding the mark in the state that he was.

At last, he gave up and said, "How can you do that and why can't I?"

The old master solemnly said, "You have learnt to focus your body, your muscles, your eyes and hence you can shoot well. But you have not yet learnt to focus your mind. Till you do it, you cannot be perfect."

☆ ☆ ☆

Many of us achieve certain levels of success in our lives, but still we find that we have not learnt to focus the mind. Success comes because we have learnt to focus a part of that energy. But if all the energy were concentrated, success that would then be attained would be beyond one's expectations.

Then, there are also some of us, who just go about in life without any aim and without any focus. We dream big, we want to achieve certain goals, but there is no focus, which leaves us struggling like blind men in a maze!

Focus to Manufacture Abundance

Focus of the mind can come by making the right choices at each moment.

Focusing is a process of remaining aware each moment so that the energy remains directed at one point or goal, and so that the concentration does not waver.

The first step in this direction is to "decide your goal". There can be no focus without an aim. Goal provides the required energy that powers our life. Ascertaining the goal means deciding which things matter most to us and then directing all our energy towards those things.

> One reason so few of us achieve what we truly want is that we never direct our focus; we never concentrate our power. Most people dabble their way through life, never deciding to master anything in particular.
>
> – Tony Robbins

Amazingly, you will find that once the goal is clear and the energy totally focused, results come faster and with minimum effort. Problems get solved with less thinking. This leads to less worries and more fulfillment and joy.

People who have achieved tremendous success have always remained focused in their work, whether it is business, sport, science or any other field for that matter. They forgot everything else, sometimes to very amusing or embarrassing consequences.

Once, Newton sat in his living room completely engrossed in some mathematical calculations. He had completely forgotten that he had invited a friend for dinner that evening. For that very reason he had also forgotten to tell his servant to set table for two.

At the right time, his friend arrived and found him totally focused in his work. So concentrated was Newton that he did not even know of his friend's presence in the room. The friend sat there silently. At last, the servant arrived with dinner for one. The friend waited for some time and then got down to the dinner. Half an hour later, Newton looked up from the papers on which he was working and was surprised to see his friend there. He was even more surprised to see the empty plate and said, "When did you come? Surprising, I did not hear you! And if it weren't for the empty plate lying there, I could have sworn that I have not yet dined."

One might well laugh at Newton for being so forgetful and absent minded. But this is the mark of a person who is totally concentrated in what he is doing! It was because of such an amazing level of focus that he went on to make such astounding discoveries which eluded the human mind for ages. Apples and so many other objects had always been falling on the ground but no one questioned why it was so or why things did not fly away into the sky.

Not just Newton, all great inventors and discoverers

were equipped with single pointed focus, which enabled them to reach conclusions that changed the very course of mankind. And not just the scientists, famous people in every field – politics, business, sport and even religion – attained to unparalleled level of success, simply because their ability to focus was phenomenal. It was only their profound ability to focus that enabled them to succeed when others with similar goals failed. What more, they achieved this success in a very short span, which once again inspires us to conclude that focus makes less more! Even the least effort in the state of total concentration leads to amazing results.

But how should one achieve total concentration?

Chapter on "Mind Over Matter" discusses this in detail. However, some useful points to remember are:

- Determine a goal and be in firm pursuit of it.
- Doubt is the enemy of focus.
- Failures, setbacks, problems are all the names of the game.
- Do not allow your fears to make the goal look distant and unachievable.
- Regular meditation is a good way of attaining the focus and keeping it intact.
- Think of your goal as often as you can.
- Imagine reaching your goal. Better still; write it to put an official stamp of commitment on it.
- Keep track of the progress and strike off your failures.

- Most importantly, when getting down to pursue your goal or putting your plans into action, channel all your energy into the task before you. Let not even a shred of that energy go waste in doubt or fear. Remember that when you eliminate fear and doubt from your mind, you have already won half the race, for, then you tend to be more confident and at the same time relaxed, allowing the hidden and obvious faculties of your mind to give their best.

> *The famous American athlete Carl Lewis, winner of 10 Olympic medals and 10 World Championship medals; hailed as the 'Sportsman of the Century' and 'Olympian of the Century' said – "My thoughts before a big race are usually pretty simple. I tell myself – Get out of the blocks, run your race, stay relaxed! If you run your race, you'll win . . . channel your energy, focus!"*

[Chapter Eight]

He who enjoys his Work, never works a day in his Life

Work is either fun or drudgery. It depends on your attitude. I like fun.

– *Colleen C. Barrett*

Doing the best at this moment puts you in the best place for the next moment.

– *Oprah Winfrey*

Three masons were at work at a construction site. A visitor to the area asked them,
"What are you doing?"
One of them replied, "Don't you see Sir, I am laying bricks."
The second mason said, "I am doing my work to earn my living."
The third one remarked, "I am building a temple."

The three answers speak for themselves. While all three masons are doing the same work, it is the third mason who is truly enjoying it. He takes pride in what he is doing. He is happy, neither tired nor bored. Others are simply exchanging their time for money and carrying the burden of duty over their heads.

Years ago I had a maid, from the eastern part of India. While working, whether it was scrubbing the floor or dusting the furniture, she smiled and sang merrily to herself. The songs she sang were in her dialect and I could not understand a word. But they touched a chord in the heart. She left me with a question, 'Is cleaning the house a misery or joy?'

Obviously, the 'job' does not contain the misery or joy. It is the people who contain it.

It is a sad commentary that a large number of people go to work because they have to. They keep on working in a routine manner, keep grumbling most of the time and ultimately choose to remain in misery. Possibly, they continue to work on the belief that work and fun are two separate things. At work, one can't have fun and enjoyment and if it's fun, then it can't be work. Well, it does not have to be that way!

Everyone has a choice. If one chooses to enjoy what one does, what is then required to be done?

Simply state and restate everything that you are against and don't like – take the responsibility to change things. If you dislike your work or are against your boss, do not allow it to become the centre of your thoughts and do not forget about improvements. If you are against a policy, think about an improved policy. If your partner's outburst upsets you, choose for your partner's gentleness. Therefore, to love what you do requires re-alignment and re-defining your thoughts. Once it is done, you do not feel the boredom, you don't feel the pain, you don't feel the misery. You work effortlessly. You enjoy your job. You enrich your life.

> Love like you have never been hurt, dance like no one is watching & work like you don't need the money.
> – *Anonymous*

It's easier said than done: What about some real issues?

For one, the work one loves might not be so financially satisfying. After all, one of the main reasons for working is earning a decent salary. Many people are forced to take up jobs against their liking, simply because what they like is not available or not be paying enough! Budding artists, actors and writers often face this dilemma.

Creative pursuits require patience and passion. You cannot pin a cloud or catch a moonbeam in your hands; either you gather all your gusto and truly go after what you want; or you pursue the most financially liberating option. Do it to the best of your ability and then alongside fulfill your creative desire. Palash Sen, leader of the music band, Euphoria is also an MBBS doctor. Why must I go far, this is my third book, and I have been a mining engineer all my life!

Another deterring factor could be the unavailability of a good opportunity. I know a well built, tall, handsome young man who looks like the best of models. But in spite of his years of trying, he has not yet landed a single modeling assignment. He has gone by the book, approached agents, good photographers and has a fantastically prepared portfolio. One cannot think of anything as to why he has not succeeded, except that it is not so destined, at least not till now! In the mean time, he has acquired a management degree and is working as manager in a business firm.

The important question is, "What should one do in such a situation?"

Should one just make efforts to find 'the dream job or work' or is there a way to love what one is already doing? Put your heart 100% into what is being done by you. Involve yourself fully. Practice "DEVOTION" in everything you do. Remember that devotion

> When there is no turning back, then we should concern ourselves only with the best way of going forward.
> – *The Alchemist, Paulo Coelho*

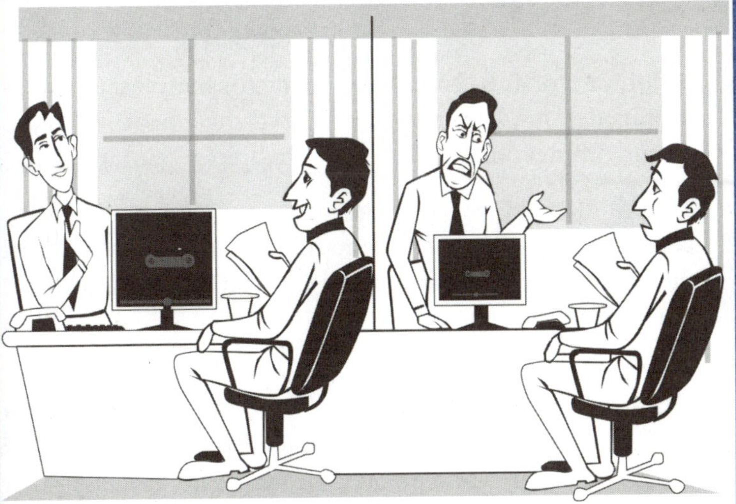

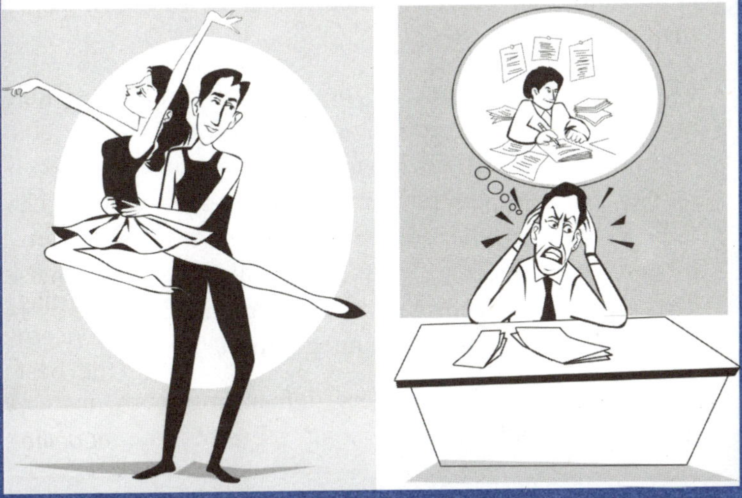

is not for worship only; it is not only for temples, mosques or gurudwaras. It should be in everything you do. All work done with devotion will result in happiness and love.

The modern day working conditions are surely very competitive, tough, and demanding. An executive in an office is expected to put in some extra bit for the betterment of the organization.

Whether one is a teacher, an executive, a doctor, a police officer or a businessperson, the growing competition and the endeavours to meet the ever rising standards of excellence keep everyone on their toes. Undoubtedly, such a working environment becomes very stressful and often makes the mind suffer. And a mind devoid of peace can never be happy.

As the world tries to move towards perfection, the stress is virtually unavoidable. When this is the case, are we all then destined to suffer?

I know two people, both of them working in a BPO. Both are young men who have compromised to take up jobs, though not of their passion and liking, because they need money. Both of them have their own dreams. One wishes to be a choreographer someday, and spends his spare time in a dance school, learning more and also teaching others. The other wants to be a fiction writer and all day, new plots keep sprouting in his fertile imagination.

The BPO industry being very demanding, both of them have to toil really hard to satisfy the customers and also their bosses. They have to face unpleasant customers daily and time to time both get a pep talk from their bosses, who do not believe in mincing words when it comes to criticizing and finding faults in an attempt to improve their performance.

Although exposed to similar situations, their approach towards work is totally different. The aspiring dancer and choreographer remains ever cheerful and takes on all comments and troubles with a positive frame of mind, genuinely trying to improve his performance. When criticized, he takes it as a suggestion having some scope for improvement. When a customer seems unsatisfied or angry, he becomes even more pleasant in his behavior and tries his best to handle things coolly. And he does it without any visible effort. As a result, at the end of the day he still has enough energy for his dancing, which he feels helps him to get rid of any accumulated stress.

The would-be-writer goes through the same grind but with a bleak outlook. He argues when criticized, loses his cool with the customers and is often seen abusing the system and the customers. He clearly seems to be an unhappy guy. He certainly shows that he hates what he is doing. This feeling of hatred and acrimony saps his energy and although after office, he very much wants to do some creative writing, he finds the going hard and is not able to spur his imagination. Because of feelings of hatred and anger, he is not left with any energy to put in the task he really loves.

I often meet both of them and find that while the former is definitely making some progress towards the achievement of his dream, the latter is neither able to do his job nor pursue his passion. Seeing them, I feel one should make the best of the opportunity and try to put in your best with a happy outlook and winning attitude.

> Happiness is not a goal,
> It is a way of travelling.
> – *William James*

The positive frame of mind would not only enable you to work better, but would also keep revitalizing you with enough energy to enable you to move forward towards the fulfillment of your dream!

In other words, happiness is a state of mind. Decide to be happy. It does not matter where you are, what you do. What matters is "How you react to a particular situation in which you are placed".

> The true way to render ourselves happy is to love our work and find in it our pleasure.
> – *Francoise de Motteville*

He who enjoys his Work, pays it forward!

I remember there were two teachers who used to teach Math to us in high school in two different sections. I changed sections in midsession and got a chance to be taught by both. The first one was a very good teacher with thorough understanding of all concepts. But the second one was truly phenomenal. He was not just clear about the concepts but he enjoyed teaching as well. The way he spoke, his body language, all were clear indicators of the pleasure he took in his work.

The concepts of integration and differentiation were very new for us and quite hard to crack. But he made it seem as if we were playing a game or solving some interesting puzzles. Even a student who was completely intimidated with Math could not remain immune to the enthusiasm he exuded. What more, when any student, weak in math got stuck at some point, he took it as a challenge. He would not go beyond the concept till every student in the class got it. There was a boy in my section, who never scored well in math. And yet, the way this teacher explained things, even he started to get good grades. Clearly, this teacher enjoyed what he was doing. There was always a smile on his face even when the class was struggling to get to the bottom of some complex concept. The end result was that the average score of our section in the yearly examination was phenomenally better than the other section.

So enjoying what you do not only makes work easier for you, but often the results are manifold. It spreads happiness and makes it better for everyone. The larger probability is that these people will make it better for the people they meet and come in contact with. And before you know it, a chain reaction of paying it forward begins. (Educationists should particularly enjoy what they do, as they are in the business of building lives.)

> Life is what we make it; always has been, always will be.
> – *Grandma Moses.*

[Chapter Nine]

Ego & Me

Ego is the biggest enemy of humans.

– *Rig Veda*

Ego has a voracious appetite, the more you feed it, the hungrier it gets.

– *Nathaniel Bronner Jr*

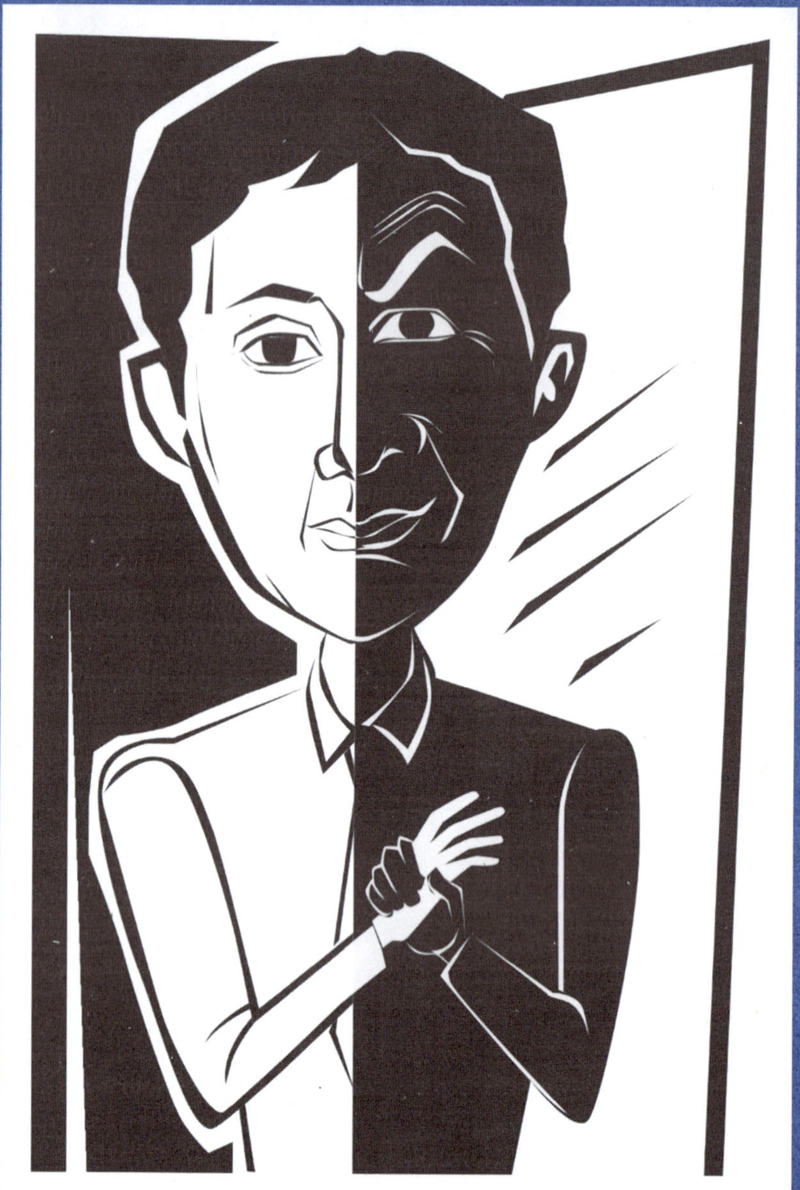

Anyone who says – "I have no ego" is an egoist in denial.

Problems can crop up in any sphere of life – at home, in a job, at a social gathering, with friends, with relatives – practically everywhere. Often if we were to trace the root cause of most of these problems, we will be led to the ego or "ahamkara". It is ego that does not let you surrender to an argument, it is ego when you can't say "I don't know", it is ego when you want to show off your knowledge and skills, it is ego when you just won't listen to another point of view because your view is the best.

Hello Mr. Egoist.

Managing ego begins with accepting that ego exists – "I have an ego. It is my sense of self-worth and I will not let it become my most prominent trait."

☆ ☆ ☆

A woman once dated two men on two consecutive evenings. On the third evening, she met a close friend, who asked how the dates went. The woman smiled and said, "After the first date, I felt I had met the most intelligent man on earth."

"So you like him?" asked her friend excitedly. "Do I at last hear the wedding bells peal?"

"No and yes!"

"What do you mean?" frowned her friend.

"Well, the answer to the first question is NO! I don't really like him. And yes, I am marrying the second guy!"

"But I thought you said the first one was the most intelligent…."

"Yes! But the second one made me feel as if I were the most intelligent woman in the world."

☆ ☆ ☆

Psyche of an egoist

I read somewhere that you often forget what someone said or did, but you never forget how he made you feel. Most of us only think of ourselves. We want to keep proving that we are the best. That might well earn us some appreciation and admiration, if we really have some worthy virtues. But if we are looking for friends and well-wishers, then our approach needs to be altogether different. Genuine appreciation only comes when we learn to put the other person first, only then, lasting relationships are built. It is easier said than done. Every human wants to feel intelligent and important, including the self. Trouble starts when you fail to see others' views, their needs and then feelings become immaterial to you. You concentrate on fulfilling only your wishes and needs. This makes it crucial to understand how to manage the self – the ego.

Ego Tactics: FEAR

A retired army colonel went in for MBA to secure a good managerial position in civilian life. And he did. He took over a garment manufacturing unit as general manager. Just a week after he had joined, the owner found him dealing with his subordinates rather rudely. He privately told him to be gentle and not to resort to his army discipline. The civilian workers may mistake his strict regimen with that of his unfair authority.

The fact is that army life requires discipline and everyone follows orders, without question because in times of emergency, any disobedience or dissent could prove counterproductive for the country. So the officers are trained to issue orders in a harsh, no-nonsense way and it is the duty of the soldiers to follow. But things are different in civilian life. In civilian life, people are at par with each other, as far as rights are concerned and no one likes being ordered around.

In spite of the owner's advice, the colonel continued with his strict ways. Only a month into his job, a section of workers rose up in revolt against his dictatorial attitude. But the colonel instead of taking this as a sign of things to come, decided to ruthlessly suppress what he thought was mutiny.

He approached some hoodlums and paid them to beat up the leader of the group. He wanted to create an atmosphere of fear and hoped that this would be a lesson to other workers too. But things backfired. The following morning, when the colonel reached his office, he was greeted by about twenty workers, who dragged him into his office, locked it and mercilessly beat him up.

Police cases were filed from both the sides. All the 150 workers in the manufacturing unit came out in support of the accused workers and they threatened to stop work, if the ex-colonel was not ousted. The owner had no choice but to comply. The arrogant and egoistical ex-army man lost not only his job but also his respect in the community.

☆ ☆ ☆

This might seem to be an extreme case, where the ego landed the manager in such deep trouble. Anyone who tries to get others to comply by instilling fear should know that tables can always get turned on him or her.

Ego Result: Inability to think right

Mahesh Chopra was a good teacher. But his problem was his anger, which he used to easily dispense at his students in school and at his kids at home. The dictum "Spare the rod and spoil the child" was his philosophy and he never faltered at that. He believed that his cane was enough to 'inspire' the erring pupil to work better. Had he thought about children and their problems, the whole school would not have feared him.

At home, his children continued to grow in fear and awe of their father. They did try to reason with him but he was never ready to listen. Though he did manage to instill fear in them, he could never earn their respect and love.

As kids, they had no option, but to follow his dictates, but things changed when they grew up. As soon as they had secure jobs, the two boys deserted him and went away to live their own lives. What more, even his own wife left him to live with one of her sons. Luckily, he had his own home and a pension.

Do you think this experience changed him?

Not a bit! He continued to be as bitter and angry as before. In fact, he opined, 'I knew these boys were good for nothing. They have only proved me right! That is why I was so strict with them. At least now they have their own jobs and are not a burden on their old father.'

Even stark experiences fail to impact us in the right way. It did not change Mahesh. Ego not only makes one lose balance in thinking, but it also makes one blind to the truths, which different experiences in life try to enlighten us to. Even when such a person loses everything that matters in his life, his ego is never satisfied.

Marriage and EGO

At a very young age, Jiya got married to a very good natured gentleman. A mining engineer by profession, soon after their marriage, her husband got posted to a project in a remote area. Even though the company accommodated them in a big bungalow, which stood in the middle of a jungle, an almost perfect getaway for the newly-weds, there was a problem.

Jiya's husband preferred spending his evening playing cards with his friends rather than being with her. As his group grew bigger, his visits to the downtown became a regular feature and he would drive miles away in his jeep, leaving Jiya to battle her loneliness and boredom all by herself. All day, he would be away for his work and in the evening, he would be away for his vocation. Jiya tried her best to cope with the situation, but the gloomy surroundings, lack of social interaction and the apathetic attitude of her husband left her struggling with depression. On one occasion she even gathered courage and talked to her husband about it. But he just laughed the matter away and continued with his uncaring ways.

His indifferent attitude pushed her to ultimate limits – she tried to commit suicide. Luck saved her! Post this episode, Jiya surely continued to live with him but there was no love, no contact, no relationship between the two and reverence, one of the most important things within a marriage, had become a thing of the past. Years later, when he died, she was not widowed, only liberated.

☆ ☆ ☆

Most of us seek a loving partner, welcoming home, lovable kids – in other words peace and happiness. But just like everything else in life, a home too needs investment. You might well build a house with all modern comforts in it with the help of money. But peace and happiness need a different kind of investment – that of love and care!

The ego took a subtler form in the case of Jiya and her husband. There were no squabbling and no financial problems in their marriage. The man was good natured. His only misdoing was that he could not give his time and express his concern to her. Quite selfishly, he only thought of his own enjoyment. The ego or self drove him to neglect his wife to the very edge of death! Though she did not leave him, their marriage died a silent death when she lost all respect for him.

In fact, it can take very small 'bouts of ego' to ruin marital bliss.

☆ ☆ ☆

Vinay and Priya Mishra both IIM graduates, had fallen in love during their academic years. Both secured enviable positions in the corporate world and soon thereafter, got married. Things went well for two years with their active social life, weekend sojourns to malls and cineplexes, and vacations in holiday spots like Switzerland and Bahamas. Relatives on both sides were pleased whenever they saw the happily married couple.

As the extended honeymoon slowly frizzled out and the reality of a married existence struck home, what surfaced was the palpable strain between them. Priya would fly off the handle over petty issues. She got a higher salary package and that lent her a false sense of superiority. She thought she was wiser of the two and expected him to go by her advice on every matter. With time, she grew insulting in her behaviour. One weekend, they invited some friends home for dinner. Vinay wanted that they should cook at home, while Priya was of the opinion that they should order food from outside. The minor issue soon became a full-fledged quarrel and in a fit of rage, Priya walked out of the house, though Vinay pleaded with her to stay. That was the end of their marriage!

☆ ☆ ☆

In the case of many couples, where both husband and wife earn; their job profiles, the difference in earnings; can prove to be a real ego battle. What one tends to forget is that they are working for their own happiness and providing for their own family, and not to prove who is superior or who can make more bucks. It takes one to be deeply humble to not mind anything that the partner does or says. But very few couples have such a rapport, and if you ever come across any such couple, take a break and observe how smoothly they avoid treading on each other's toes (read ego).

EGO @ WORK

While ego does affirm a boss' ability to take charge, checking the ego demonstrates his ability to take charge of himself. Undoubtedly, the boss has to believe in himself, otherwise no one else will. His conviction in his own abilities has to be very strong and resilient too. But such a self assurance should not be allowed to become arrogance. The motto is use your ego, but do not allow your ego to use you.

Once this happens, the results at work include better understanding, camaraderie and profits.

On the contrary, Mr. Egoist will always show one-up-manship; he will show that he is more intelligent than others; he will express personal antagonism; he will force his way and create confusion. The egoist argues for the sake of argument and to show the other person down. In the process, the end objective is not achieved.

Here are three tips to keep your ego in check:

i) Accept praise, but never believe it totally.

ii) Always listen to your best friend, be it your colleague or spouse. Such friends are not afraid to give each other the straight dope.

iii) Always take time out to reflect and do an open assessment of your shortcomings.

Based on experience, given below are five points to achieve success at work without bringing ego to the fore:

i) State the objective clearly.

ii) Write down the Facts and Figures.

iv) Invite ideas to achieve the objective (these ideas may even be written and handed over to avoid ego battles between employees).

v) Without ego, choose the best idea.

vi) Make a strategy to implement the best idea.

EGO & U

Learning to isolate Ego from you is the struggle that we all must undertake.

★ ★ ★

A famous monastery with over hundred disciples had two wings. Half of the disciples lived in the right wing and

> Make a decision to relinquish the need to control, the need to be approved, and the need to judge. Those are the three things the ego is doing all the time.
> – Deepak Chopra

the remaining half in the left wing. There was a pet cat in the monastery and a dispute rose as to who should own the cat – the right wing or the left wing? What began as an argument took the form of an ugly quarrel, till matters came to such a pass that disciples of the two wings were ready to fly at each others' throats. Just in the nick of time, the master intervened and ordered the disciples to calm down or leave the monastery. When he heard the dispute, he could not help pitying them for their foolishness. To test them and teach them a lesson he said, "Fine! This is my decision. Cut the cat into two halves and each wing can keep one half. Go and bring a sword."

To his surprise all agreed. The sword was brought. As he raised it to strike the cat, a voice called out, "Stop!"

The master was relieved. He looked up only to find an 11-year-old boy who had just joined the monastery a month ago, looking at him in rage.

"What is it you want?" said the master.

"Are you really going to cut the cat?" asked the boy.

"Yes, of course!" said the master.

"Then I am leaving. I was told you are a great master.

You are all a bunch of fools here – the master as well as the disciples. You are putting a poor creature to pain just because of your foolish prides."

The master called the boy forward and hugged him. Legend says that the boy went on to become a great Tao master, who helped many go beyond the ego.

☆ ☆ ☆

The story might or might not be true. You might even smile and say that no one would be that foolish to divide a cat by cutting it up. But if we look carefully, we go on making impossible demands of others just because of the ego. Only the boy thought of the pain of the cat. He thought of the cat, unlike the rest of the disciples who were only bothered about becoming masters of the cat! The cat in this story represents happiness which the disciples derived by petting and caring for the pet. The ego believed in having all happiness for itself instead of sharing it with others, even if it meant destroying the very source of that happiness. Certainly not the way of the wise! So be wise and don't cut up your cat!

Instead, learn to say 'shut up' to the ego which keeps crying – I, mine, only me! The ego might well earn you some moments of false pride and joy, but if you learn to switch it off, you will earn lasting peace and happiness not only for yourself but for others too.

[Chapter Ten]

The Art of Giving

"The value of a man resides in what he gives and not in what he is capable of receiving."
— *Albert Einstein*

"Think of giving not as a duty but as a privilege."
— *John D. Rockefeller*

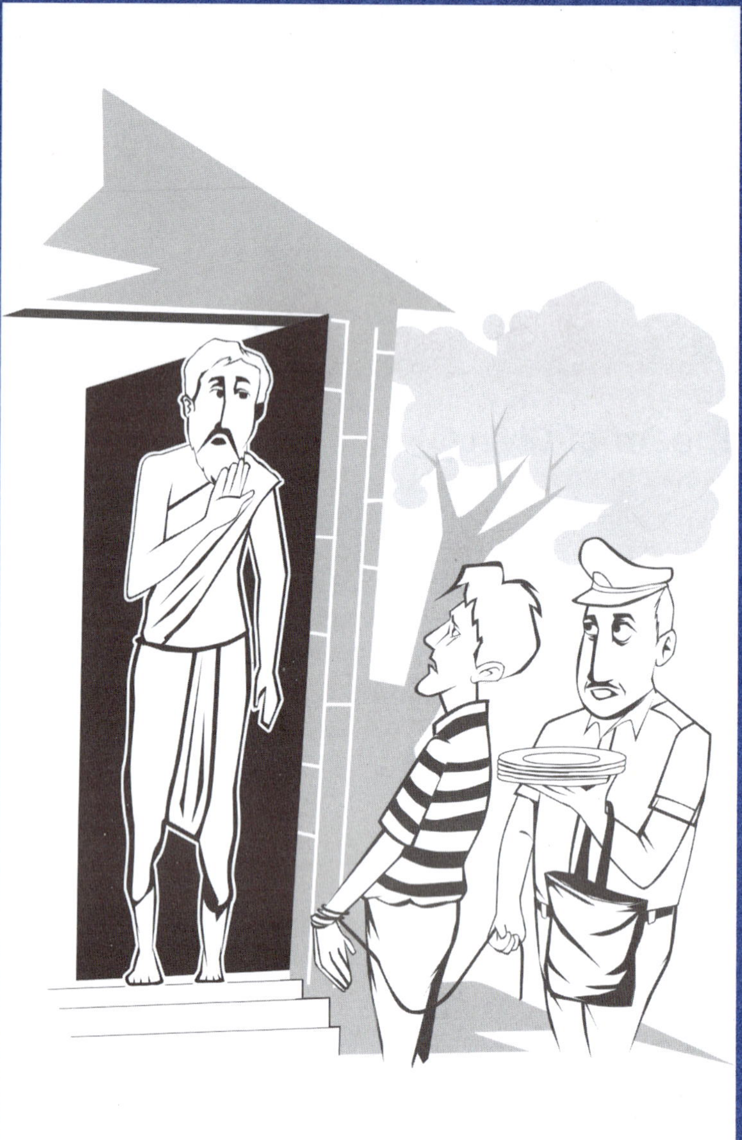

Ten-year-old Ajay was all ears with rapt attention, as his father continued, "It was night and the priest in his kind manner, offered food and shelter to the thief. The thief saw the silver plates in which the food was served to him and felt tempted to steal them. After dinner, he tried to sleep but could not. In the stillness of the night, he got up from his bed and tiptoed to the kitchen".

"What was he up to?" asked Ajay, looking wide-eyed and restless.

"Just listen," said his father. "About an hour later, some people banged the main door of the priest's house very loudly. The priest opened the door. He found a police inspector and three constables standing with the thief, his hands cuffed. The police inspector informed the priest that they found six silver plates in the thief's bag. He claims that you have given it to him," the inspector told the priest.

"The priest at once confirmed that this was true. Convinced by the priest's answer, the police inspector released the thief and handed over the silver plates to him. As soon as the police departed; the thief, who felt highly ashamed, fell to

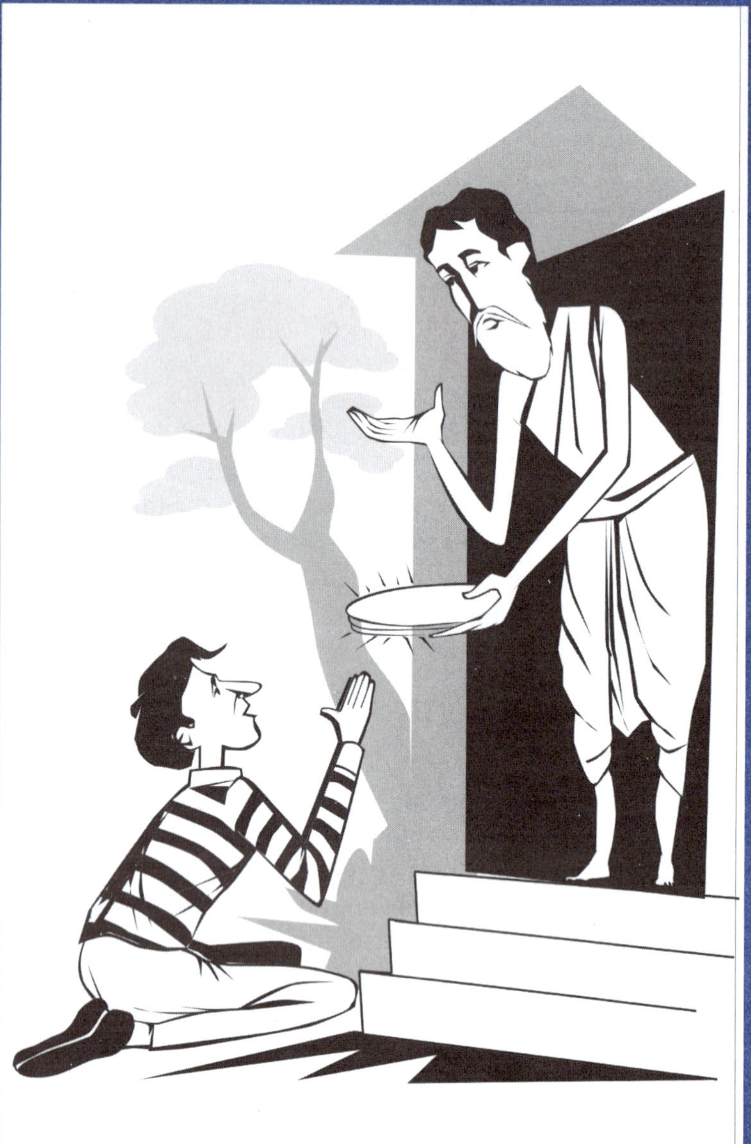

the priest's feet and started weeping. The priest raised him to his feet and hugged him. The thief was in utter disbelief and surprise. The thief said sorry and thanked the priest. He was giving the silver plates back to him. But the priest said, 'You need them. That is why you took them. So you may keep them.'"

The thief, ashamed of his act, repeatedly begged to be excused and insisted that the priest take back the plates. But the priest said, "Please keep the plates as a gift from me. But give me something in return if you can." The bewildered thief asked what he could possibly give to the priest. The priest surprised him when he said, "Promise that you will never steal again." The thief swore that he would live an honest life from then on, but insisted that the priest take back the plates.

The priest said, "How will you lead an honest life? You will need money to start some business. Keep these plates, go and make an honest living." The thief thanked him and left.

"The priest was kind, he excused the thief and saved him from the police," said little Ajay. "But why did he not take back the silver plates? They belonged to him."

Ajay's dad said, "By giving generously and not as an obligation, he made him feel the pain. It hurt the 'thief' so much that he is now on his journey of an honest and happy living."

Ajay pondered and then asked, "Dad! Should I also do the same with Vikas? He keeps stealing my things at school.

Our madam has scolded him many a times but he doesn't listen. Can we also change him this way?"

"Sure! It is worth trying," said Ajay's father, handing over a packet of some new erasers, pencils and a ruler to him.

On his return from office the following day, he found his son very excited and beaming. "It worked dad! Vikas was astounded when I gave him the new things. He apologized and promised never to steal again. He even said that he would return back my things."

☆ ☆ ☆

Osho says that a servant steals not because he lacks moral fiber, but because he lacks money. He prophesized that the rich should consider themselves nothing more than custodians and not owners of the wealth that has fallen to their share. Not only this, they should even focus to part with it in as much measure as possible. In reality,

"The more you give, the more you get. Moreover, you get what u give."

When can you truly give & what is the difference you want to make

> When one is out of touch with oneself, one cannot touch others.
>
> – *Anonymous*

When you love yourself, when you are contended, when you respect yourself, you can give birth to your best self and then you can give abundantly. You can give the gift of your heart that touches and honours the other person. You will then give with your heart rather than the head. **The key is to give to our self first and be contended.** The greatest gift, we can give to anyone is the gift of our self.

Kahlil Gibran wrote, "You give but little when you give of your possessions. It is when you give of yourself that you truly give."

In other words, we cannot truly give unless we ourselves are full. Moreover, it is difficult to be sensitive to others misfortunes if you are empty yourself.

When to GIVE

No one knows what will greet them the next moment – a casualty or a celebration! So the best time to give is now!

☆ ☆ ☆

Mark Twain once happened to attend a charitable meeting where the speaker, espousing the cause to the audience moved Twain so much that he decided to contribute 100 dollars for such a worthy cause. But the speaker kept procrastinating his dialogue for half an hour which ultimately led a bored and tired Twain to shell out only 50 dollars. As time passed, the amount he had in mind kept dwindling, till he finally decided to give only 10 dollars. At last, the speaker stopped speaking and the open charity box was passed around. When it reached Mark Twain, he promptly took a dollar from the box, pocketed it and passed on the box to the next person.

A funny anecdote one might think! But then this is how the mind actually works. The more you postpone things, the more reluctant the mind becomes to do anything. And when it comes to parting with money and worldly possessions, the mind needs but the slightest excuse to shy away from giving. Can there be any better excuse than postponement?

For the mind that postpones, tomorrow never comes!

How much to GIVE

Kindness in words creates confidence.

Kindness in thinking creates profoundness.

> I have found the paradox that if you love until it hurts, there can be no more hurt, only more love.
> – *Mother Teresa*

Kindness in giving creates love.

Giving is actually nothing but a gesture of love. Give till it hurts!

Experience the joy of giving. To do so, we need not be heroic. All we need to do is to awaken, to become aware of those around us. Every encounter is an opportunity and once you open up your heart, you will feel that there is really no limit to how much you can give. You will give as much as you can.

☆ ☆ ☆

Once Henry Ford was in Ireland for a vacation. Public glare follows all rich and famous even in their private vacations and so, when he was only a few days into his vacation, a person approached him and requested for donation for building an orphanage. Ever the philanthropist, Ford took out his cheque book and filled in an amount of two thousand pounds.

The news soon hogged the public attention in a local newspaper but with a typo of an extra zero. Two thousand pounds got published as twenty thousand pounds! The person, who had received the donation, rushed to Ford, humbly apologized and promised a corrigendum from the newspaper. But Ford smiled and said, "Don't do that!" He quietly fished out the cheque book from his pocket and wrote out another cheque for eighteen thousand pounds.

☆ ☆ ☆

Super rich people parting with a little chunk of their wealth – no big deal, you may say. But more than wealth, it is about giving with your heart.

☆ ☆ ☆

An old man was once summoned before a judge in a criminal court. His offence? He had stolen a loaf of bread for his starving family members. The verdict of the judge was, "The law does not discriminate and hence there is no option but to punish you. You have to pay five dollars as fine. But as you do not have a penny, I will do this on your behalf."

Having said so, the judge pulled out a five dollars note and settled the fine. He went on to say, "It is unforgivable that a man living in such a big city cannot be given even a loaf of bread by its citizens. So everyone present in this room is hereby fined a dollar." When the poor old man walked out of the court half an hour later, he was carrying fifty dollars in his pocket!

☆ ☆ ☆

You don't have to be super rich to give.

> If you can't feed a hundred people, then just feed one.
> – *Mother Teresa*

What to GIVE

It takes little to relax a tense atmosphere. Whenever we speak of giving, invariably the mind thinks of money, when actually a very small gesture can win friends and admirers in strange places.

> If you have much, give of your wealth, if you have little, give of your heart.
> – *an Arabian saying*

☆ ☆ ☆

It was in the famous Hindi movie, Munnabhai MBBS where the endearing gesture of jadu ki jhappi (hug of love) became popular. Munna, a criminal, uses unfair means to get himself enrolled in a medical college. Naturally, he is not liked by his teachers but with his adorable ways, he endears himself to the staff, right from the nurses to the janitors, with his *jaddu ki jhappi*.

It may be difficult hugging everyone and anyone in real life situations, but we surly can make a small gesture of warmth and love – a smile, a wave of hand, a nod of appreciation.

☆ ☆ ☆

Open your heart to compassion. Benevolence is actually a way of connecting with the world around you. Normally, our self-centered tendency closes us to the world and its wonders. Giving helps us bond with others. And if you have nothing more than a smile or a kind word, then go ahead. Share with others what you have. An un-giving person is like a larva trapped in a cocoon, while one who gives liberally is like a honey bee freely flying about, sprinkling around pollen and gathering sweet juices of various flowers.

Note that the greatest thing one can give is love! Charity, kind words, compassion are all but expressions of love. Most of us only worry about what we get from others. But if we care to pause a bit in our lives and decide to start giving, we would find that life has gained a new meaning. Do it today…

Try giving a flower to your boss who you think is never satisfied with your work.

Try giving a smile to the guard standing outside your colony.

Try uttering a few kind words to those working for you.

And if someone is in need of something material, then don't let that opportunity slip by. Do give something, if you can. All of a sudden, you will feel elevated, as if you are one with all those around you.

This supreme feeling of oneness is the sole reason why great avatars like Ram, Krishna and Jesus gave lavishly the hardest thing to give – forgiveness. Ram would have absolved Ravan if he returned his wife Sita, Krishna was ready to pardon Duryodhan. Jesus sought forgiveness from God for those who put him on the cross! Forgiveness is perhaps the highest expression of love and perhaps the hardest action to perform. We sulk under the feeling of hurt and nurse grudges for years, a scar that only harms and deepens with time but we refuse to forgo. Only if we knew how to exonerate, we would not linger under the burden of animosity.

Giving is a wonderful human trait that frees us of lower worlds namely greed, jealousy, animosity and attachment; and elevates us to the higher worlds like compassion, love, universal brotherhood and selflessness. It matters not what you give, for the very act of giving elevates the human soul.

> Let us not be satisfied with just giving money. Money is not enough, money can be got, but they (the people) need your hearts to love them. So, spread your love everywhere you go.
>
> – *Mother Teresa*

How to GIVE

Just as you need a generous heart to give, you need a compassionate soul to bring about a happy charity or an act of giving. The giver must give with grace and not feel proud by giving. At the same time, he must ensure that the receiver does not feel humiliated. We must not regard giving as an obligation. It is actually a desire and does as much good, if not more to the giver as the one who receives.

☆ ☆ ☆

My childhood memory of seeing my neighbour's grandmother giving away gifts was not so happy. She would stand at a 'safe' distance and ask the poor woman to spread out the end of her sari so that she would gingerly throw the items into it, taking care lest she touched her. This was a ritual she practiced with the garbage picker every festival.

I always felt bad at this discrimination and once asked her the reason for her rudeness. The reply shocked me. She proclaimed herself as an upper caste woman, who will not come near a low caste untouchable woman!

Years later, Swami Vivekanand's words calmed my restless mind that was still trapped with the grandmother's misdoings. He said, "Do not stand on a high pedestal and take 5 cents in your hand and say, 'here, my poor man', but be grateful that the poor man is there, so by making a gift to him you are able to help yourself. It is not the receiver that is blessed, but it is the giver. Be thankful that you are allowed to exercise your power of benevolence and mercy in the world, and thus become pure and perfect."

☆ ☆ ☆

Remember, the one who is giving must remain humble and behave with humility. One who is receiving already feels inferior because he has less than you. So, humility on your part assures him that giving is a gesture of love and compassion, rather than one of superiority. Infact, Indian scriptures say that any charity given with the expectation of even a 'thanks' is not true charity.

Whom to GIVE

What do you call someone who gives and donates liberally? A philanthropist. It is a Greek word formed by the conjunction of two words - philos which means love and anthropos which means humanity. So philanthropy originally means loving humanity. We love our human brethrens and hence we give. Likewise, everyone deserves to be loved and all expect love, then how can we make any distinction when it comes to giving?

Many a times, I have heard people say that we should give only to the deserving. But how do you decide the one in need?

☆ ☆ ☆

Once I was driving with a friend to some place, when at a red light a woman holding an infant approached my car and tapped on the window. As I lowered the glass pane, she started unburdening her woes upon me while tears streaked down her face.

"My child is ill. I took him to a doctor," she said, unfolding a piece of paper. It was a medical prescription. "I need some money for his medicine."

"How much will the medicine cost?" I asked, touched by her plight.

"Hundred rupees!"

Quietly, I fished out a hundred rupee note from my purse and gave it to her. She walked away, thanking me profusely.

"What did you do that for?" said my friend seated beside me, looking quite horrified. "She is a fraud. Beggars these days play this ruse to dupe people."

I smiled at her and said, "What if she really needs it?"

"I can bet she just tricked you!" exclaimed my friend with some anger.

"Could be," I said. "But I believed her and gave the money."

"For all we know, she might use your money to buy alcohol for her drunkard husband," argued my friend.

"Maybe; But I gave because I feel satisfied and happy when I help someone. It does not really matter what she does with the money. My job is to give, not to judge others."

"You are living in a make believe world. Utopia does not exist dear."

☆ ☆ ☆

I pondered over her comment and said, "Never in the history of mankind has utopia become a reality. But have we given up trying? Don't we keep making efforts to improve the world we are living in? We all know that when they grow up many kids are going to lie and be dishonest. But that does not stop us from teaching them about morality. We can just act, we cannot control the outcomes.

By trying to decide whether a person deserves to be given something, we wish to control what he or she does with it. I would say, if you find joy in giving, do it without worrying about its outcome.

Consider this: Nature has no rules of reservation for giving. The sun shines equally for a poor man, rich man, thief and even for a murderer. It never demarcates deserving from non-deserving to cast his sunshine on him. And that is the secret of its abundance. The all omnipotent also does not reason before showering us with the money that comes into our hands. Then who has given us the right to judge others?

How do you feel after GIVING

A rich mother was scolding her teenage son. "We spend so much on you. We have given you everything. But you don't care about the sacrifice we make," The boy stood there looking rather confused.

When the boy had left, an old man who was present there, came and said to her, "Never speak thus to your son. What you do is your duty! In fact, a poor woman who has just one piece of bread and gives it all to her hungry kid at the cost of starving herself, makes a bigger sacrifice than a rich person who spends a part of his large wealth on his children."

☆ ☆ ☆

I believe that the material things of the world do not belong to any one person or being. If by fate or by virtue of hard work, some wealth has fallen to one's share, one must think that one is just the custodian. For the time being, it is in one's custody. But it actually belongs to all. And when one gives with this feeling, one remains humble and the false pride of a giver does not creep into one's attitude.

On an esoteric note: We Indians are often made to believe that everything is God. All beings are the forms of God. So to whom one is giving? God! And who is giving? Again God! And in fact, one is not giving or taking, one is just sharing what actually belongs to all.

"Life is more accurately measured by the lives you touch, than by the things you acquire."

Happy sharing.

[Chapter Eleven]

Fume-mitigation
Managing Anger

For every minute you remain angry, you give up sixty seconds of your peace of mind.
— *Ralph Waldo Emerson*

The size of a man can be measured by the size of the thing that makes him angry.

Anger is like a double edged knife which hurts the source more than its victim. Ultimately it is 'you' who is losing the most when you get angry. If you are patient in one moment of anger, you will escape a hundred days of sorrow.

☆ ☆ ☆

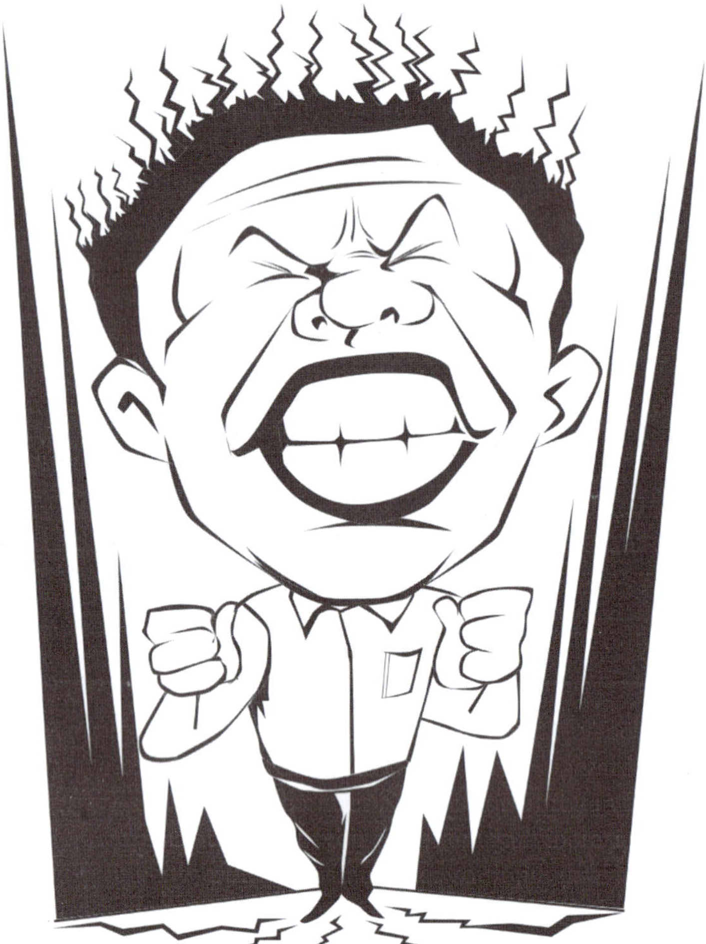

There lived a Zen master who was famed to have led more disciples to the portals of enlightenment than anyone else. A man once approached him and said, "I have heard a lot about you. But I won't be your disciple until you solve a problem I have been facing all my life."

"What is it?" asked the master.

"Well, I simply can't control my anger. When I lose my temper, everyone fears to approach me. I have lost so much in life because of this. Even my wife has left me."

The master said, "That is a very unique problem you have. Fine, let me see your anger."

The man looked confused and said, "But your holiness, how can I show it to you?"

"You said you cannot control your anger," said the master. "So, if it is yours show it to me."

"It comes all of a sudden. I have no control over it." The man argued.

"Then that means it is not yours, otherwise you could have shown it to me at will."

The man irritatingly said, "Please don't play with words. Tell me if you can help me get rid of it?"

"Anger is not a part of your true nature," said the master. "Just think! Was there anger in your nature when you were born? All I can do is, show you your true nature. And when you see your true nature, anger will disappear on its own."

☆ ☆ ☆

For years, I had carried the baggage of anger on my shoulders – anger that invariably left me seething and disturbed. Though I knew nurturing it would be fatal, yet I lived with this ordeal for years.

Let us say it out–loud, **"Anger is not a part of my nature."** Say it twice.

Believe it.

The Birth of Anger

My earliest childhood memories bring back the angry scowling face of my father. He had a mercurial temper. And anyone including our close relatives, who ever had to face his brunt felt, "Better not face him when he is angry."

Whenever I heard his voice rising above the normal decibel, a strange fear gripped my little heart. Though, he never shouted at me yet I would act docile and never try to do anything that would incur his displeasure. I had become acquainted with his anger ever since his wrath was unleashed upon others. So wisely, I 'learnt' to do things in a manner that my father considered 'right', which included studying hard, scoring good marks, not giggling or laughing unnecessarily and not listening to loud music. What more, every time he lost his cool at someone, I would cringe. Even when he was angry at others, I felt it was my fault. I felt it was my responsibility to placate him with my good behaviour.

Slowly his personality started to rub off on me. I was becoming an angry person just like him. His voice seemed to ring within me all the time, telling me what was right and what was wrong. Whenever I wanted to do something, a voice in my head would tell me how my father would have liked me to act. And my robotic impulse gave responses that he liked. Was it an 'inheritance' of anger from him or an unconsciously programmed behavior to lead life as he wished? The accumulation of pent up unexpressed emotions, feelings and wishes in me, were actually cracking me up and I was done up beautifully to explode.

Adulthood got me in contact with the outer world and as I distanced myself from home, particularly my father, I noticed that this trigger mechanism / anger bothered me. Feeling angry was not my character but my father's trait that I was conditioned to implement. And I did! But every time I lost my cool, I felt abysmally bad about it. This upset me a great deal, caused me pain and aches, and left me totally disturbed.

I decided to take control before it took control of me. I began to realize that I harboured anger because I stayed in its habitat.

Let me say it out-loud, **"I am not an angry person."** Say it twice.

Believe it.

Anger Triggers

A boss's annoyance is usually directly proportional to work. Likewise children throw tantrums if they do not get what they want. We as adults blow our tops when our wishes are not fulfilled. In every situation, **unfulfilled expectations** trigger anger.

Mistakes of others and also our own make us angry. A bus driver loses his cool when a biker speeds past him dangerously. A man curses someone who steps on his toes and a housewife gets angry at the maid for breaking an expensive crystal. A student gets angry at himself for having committed an error in the exam.

One can also get emotionally sparked off in **testing moments**; like a person may unleash his anger at God if he suffers from a life threatening ailment like cancer. A boy being bullied at school for many weeks continuously could suddenly retaliate out of brewing frustration.

On the contrary, anger is not always a response to unsatisfactory situations! Sometimes it is **used to instill fear and make others obey**. Bosses use

> Anger is an acid that can do more harm to the vessel in which it is stored than to anything on which it is poured.
>
> – Mark Twain

it, and so do parents and even teachers! While most of us might use it to get work done in a satisfactory manner, some people use it to feel powerful.

☆ ☆ ☆

A ten-year-old boy had a nasty temper. At the slightest provocation, he would fly into a rage and break things in his destructive spree. Later, he would feel repentant, but would forget all about it when thrown into a testing situation again.

One day, he pleaded with his father, "You scolded me many a times, counseled me and even spoke to me about my raging fury. What should I do to get rid of my anger?"

"Till you do not understand how gravely anger harms you, you will not be able to stop it. Let me think about it and find some way out for you," the father explained.

In the evening, the father returned home with a big heart made of wood. He gave it to his son and said, "Each time you feel angry, drive a nail into this heart."

"How will this help?" asked his son, with some curiosity.

"Just do it and you will see for yourself?"

The first day, the boy drove no less than ten nails into the heart. This went on for many days. The boy soon realised that driving a nail into the wood was not such an easy task. The effort left him tired. His mind told him that it was better if he could avoid driving in nails somehow. So each time he got angry, he was reminded of the tough task ahead. Slowly, the number of nails going into the wooden heart became lesser and soon a time came when the boy did not lose his temper even once in a day, then a week and finally a month. Awestruck by his son's feat, his father asked him if his advice worked.

"Yes," said the proud son. "I no longer get angry."

"Get me the wooden heart with the nails," said the father.

"I don't even know where it is. I have not used it for over a month. Do you really need it?"

"Yes, there is still one more lesson for you to learn. Also bring the pliers from the tool box."

The boy soon returned with the pliers and the wooden board. The father pulled out the nails one by one. When all the nails were pulled out, he held up the wooden heart and said, "Imagine this board to be your heart. Every bout of anger pierced it and made a hole in it. And these holes are nothing but scars. **A few moments of anger can scar our entire lives.**"

☆ ☆ ☆

Good Anger, Bad Anger

Anger is a feeling of displeasure or hostility. It is an unpleasant emotion, but it's also a normal, healthy emotion. When you feel something is not right, it is often natural to show one's disapproval. Moreover, anger is a natural response to perceived threats.

> Anyone can become angry – that is easy, but to be angry with the right person at the right time, and for the right purpose and in the right way – that is not within everyone's power.
>
> – *Aristotle*

Anger becomes a problem only when you don't manage it in a healthy way.

If there is injustice and one feels inclined to protest, then this emotion should not be restrained. Suppressing one's feelings and emotions also proves detrimental to one's physical and mental health. Psychologists strongly recommend that one should not let emotions pent up. They need a release. At the same time, it is advised that one clears up matters in a firm but calm manner. In a given situation, expression of anger knowingly is an expression of intelligence and gives peace. But if it is unwarranted, it gives deep pain and unhappiness.

Ultimately, anger affects. It affects the health, the mind and even takes a toll on one's relationships. If there is one sure way of losing a friend, it is anger. If there is one sure way of distancing oneself from others, it is anger. Anger mars friendship and creates wide bridges. So use anger with discretion and with due thought.

FUME-MITIGATION: How to mitigate anger?

Our experiences in life help us formulate our own ways to manage anger. But there are some time tested ways to fume-mitigate.

- Not reacting instantly is a good way to manage anger. Watch anger, understand anger, become aware of anger. Don't do anything. Just let it be there. Look deep into it. Very soon, you would observe anger starts transforming into compassion. This is the most important moment. This is the key. It is just the awareness that does everything for you. The energy/wisdom that we need to achieve this is just mindfulness/awareness. Please note that with the awareness, it is not that we have controlled our anger. But we are patient. We are patient because hatred has become love. And always remember, patience is a by-product of inner bliss and leads to infinite happiness.

- Meditation is a good means of learning how to perfect the art of achieving awareness and then managing anger. A few meditative moments with self can be extremely helpful.

- Developing an empathetic attitude towards others can help prevent anger. To err is human, to forgive divine! Understanding the fact that people can make mistakes and it is but natural to do so, will help one be calmer.

- A good sense of humour helps one sail smoothly through various testing situations of life. Humour not only eases volatile situations, it ceases negativity to surface. Words meant to convey positive criticism may be taken in a healthy spirit if used with a humourous pill.

- A positive attitude towards circumstances and people helps conserving energy. This redirected energy could be used for a constructive purpose and solving problems at hand in an amicable manner.

> It is wise to direct your anger towards problems – not people; to focus your energies on answers – not excuses.
> – *William Arthur Ward*

[Chapter Twelve]

Forgiveness

To forgive is to set a prisoner free and discover that the prisoner was you.
  – *Lewis Benedictus Smedes in his book* Forgive and Forget

The weak can never forgive. Forgiveness is the attribute of the strong.

– *Mahatma Gandhi*

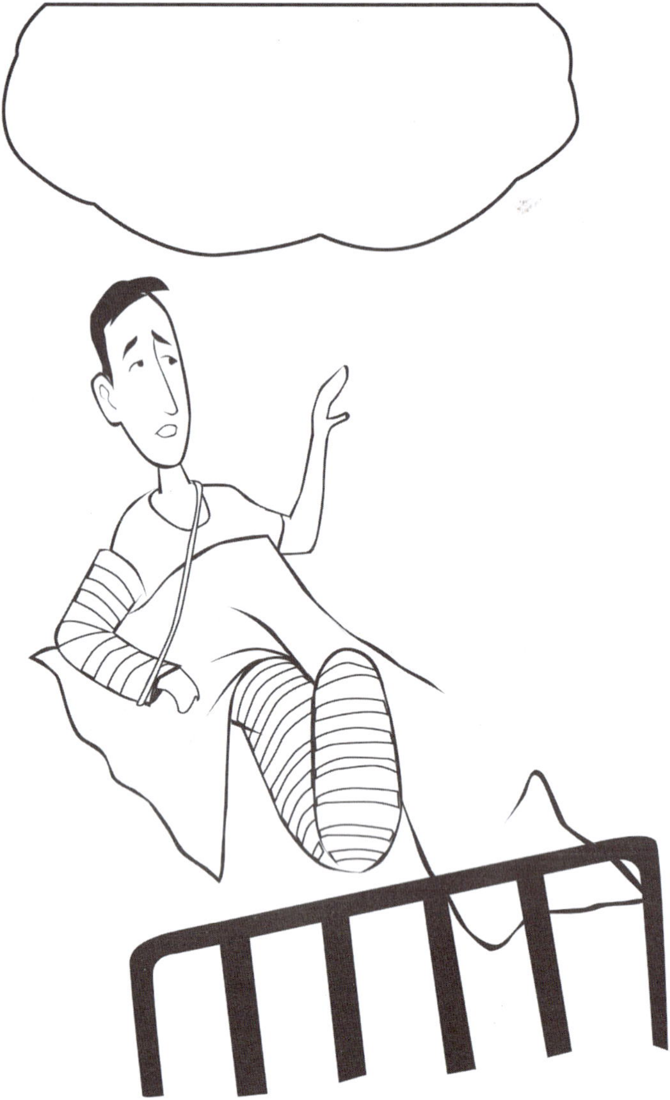

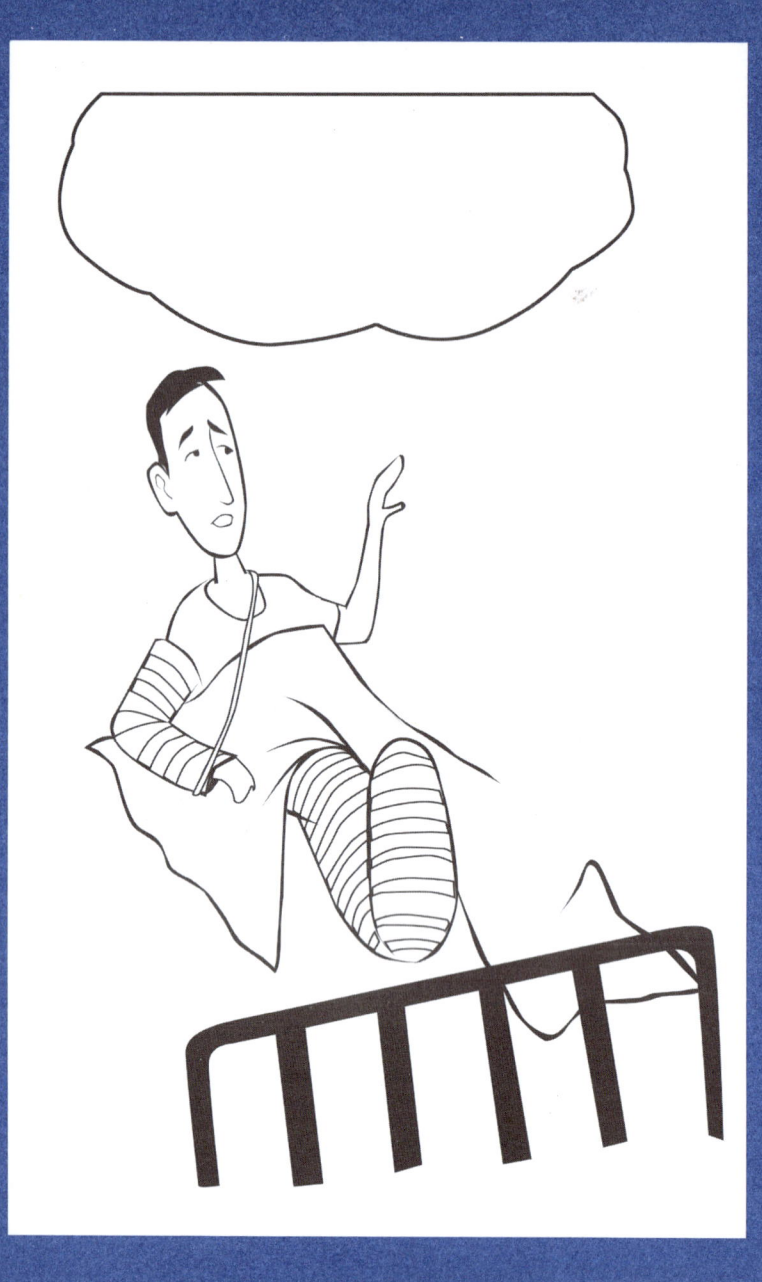

I remember reading the story of a young boy who moved with his family to a new city because of his father's transferable job. He was studying in second year for a bachelor's degree. In the new city, he got admission in a reputed college. But on the very first day at college, he became a victim of ragging. The entire incident that should have been nothing more than a prank turned ugly when the boys who were ragging him became violent. In an attempt to escape them, the boy rushed down a flight of stairs and lost his balance. Hours later, he woke up in a hospital to realize he had multiple fractures in his right leg and arm. The doctors did their best, but the surgery left him permanently handicapped for life with a limp in his leg and disfigured left arm. The dream of the boy to join the army was brutally shattered.

The rowdy boys responsible for his condition were rusticated from the college and had to face criminal charges. The court sentenced all four of them to two years in prison. But the victim could never forgive the foursome for destroying his life. He always carried resentment in his heart, and became a mere shadow of his past vivacious

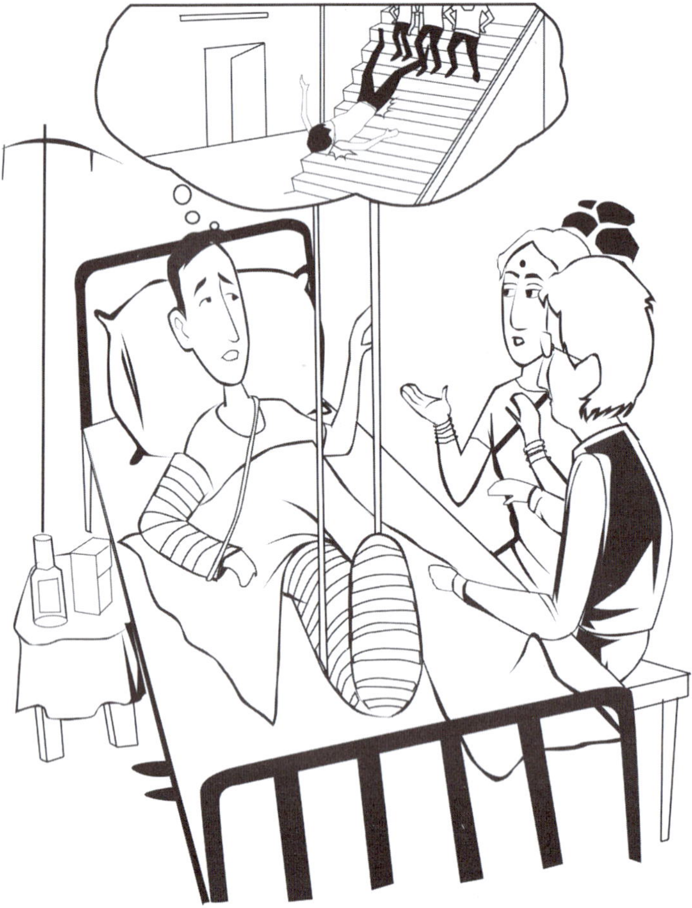

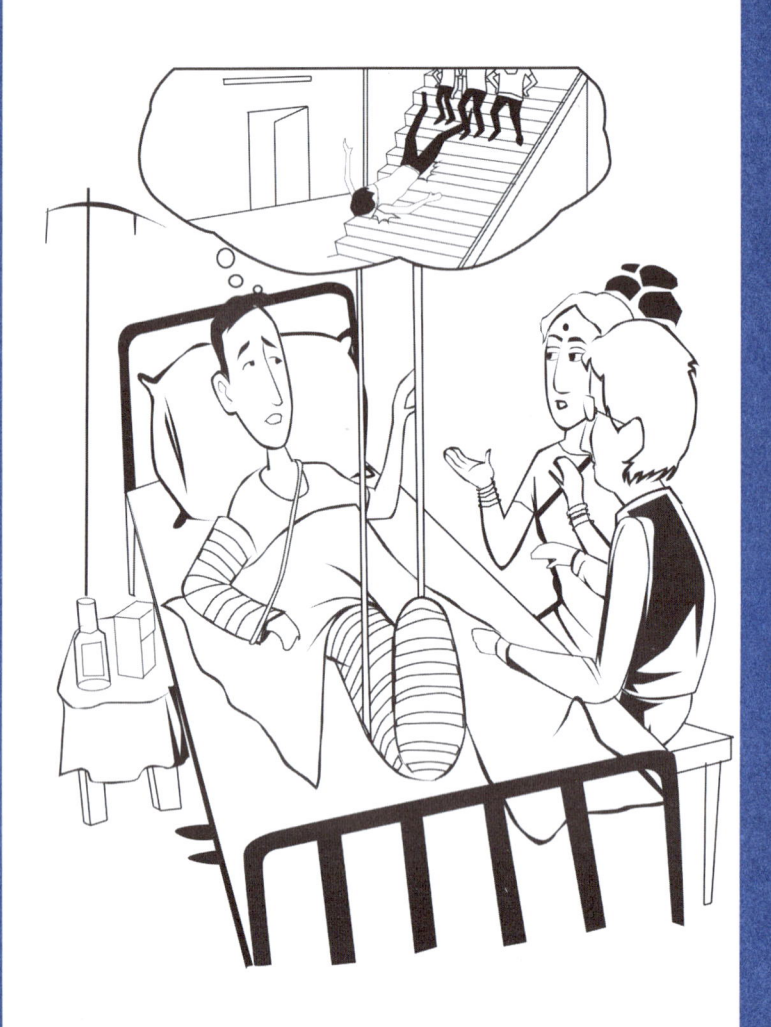

self. He lost all interest in his studies and barely managed to pass the examination to earn a bachelor's degree.

No amount of consolation from his parents and friends could help him overcome the tragedy. The repeated advice from his family members and friends to forget the incident and move on in life, did not bring any change in his thinking. One thing he just could not do – "forget and forgive the four villains" who had shattered his dreams. Their faces haunted him day and night, and he seethed within always. With these thoughts brewing inside him all the time, he became totally frustrated, bitter, disillusioned and revengeful.

Then one day, he just left home without telling anyone, not knowing where to go and what to do. His aimless wanderings took him to a mountain retreat towards the Himalayas. The place was beautiful, but it did little to calm his disturbed mind. One day, he stood on the edge of a precipice looking down. It was a steep fall of more than 300 meters. Suddenly, a powerful thought caught his imagination and in his dreams he had almost stepped forward to take the plunge. Just then, a strong hand caught hold of him from the back. He turned around to find an old Sadhu (priest) standing there. The first thing that struck him was the immense peace on the Sadhu's face.

A few minutes later, both of them were seated on a rock, with the boy narrating what had happened to him about three years ago and how he felt an undying fury for the four who had destroyed his life.

When the boy had finished with his story, the old Sadhu did not speak for a long time. His eyes seemed to be searching for something in the sky. At last, he broke his silence and said, "Tell me son! Do you like thinking of the four boys who hurt you or the unfortunate incident that left you with a limp?"

"Why would I like to think of them?" the boy replied in surprise.

"But this is exactly what you have been doing all along. A part of you wants to forget it all, but another part makes you cling to the past. This is a very strong link that you have forged over years and it is not allowing you to look beyond that incident."

It was the first time someone had reached so deep into his soul. The boy said, "You are right! I wish I could forget. But I can't. I am always thinking of revenge. I want to beat them and break their legs, so that they understand what they did to me. You are a holy man. Can you help me in some way?"

"Yes, I can. There is a way."

"What is it?"

"Forgive those boys."

"What? Forgive them? They, who destroyed my life? I can never do that."

"Then there is no hope for you. I am suggesting you to forgive them not for their sake. It is for your own sake.

A part of you wants to get rid of all that pain but by constantly thinking of revenge, you are making the bond of enmity stronger each day. It will ultimately destroy you. Don't have any pity for the four boys. But do have some pity for yourself. Forgive them not because you feel kind towards them, but because you want to get rid of a haunting experience that is poisoning your mind. Forgiveness will quieten your anger and resentment. Forgiveness will clear your mind and body of thoughts and feelings of the past incident. Forgiveness will enable you to enjoy the present. Forgiveness will get you what you want. Forgiveness will free you of your troubled past forever and you will be able to see that life still has so much to offer to you. Only forgiveness will give you abiding happiness."

The words acted like a balm on his bruised soul. The boy closed his eyes and spoke out the words of forgiveness. Instantly, he felt as if he had been released from bondage. Minutes later, when he opened his eyes, he smiled to see what a beautiful place he was in. He thanked the old Sadhu, bowed to him and walked away to lead a life free of the ghosts of his past.

When I had finished reading this real life story, words of the inspirational author Catherine Ponder flashed in my mind, "When you hold resentment toward someone, you are bound to that person or that condition by an emotional link, that is stronger than steel. Forgiveness is the only way to dissolve that link and get free."

The act of forgiveness freed the boy of the resentment and anger he had been carrying within for so many years.

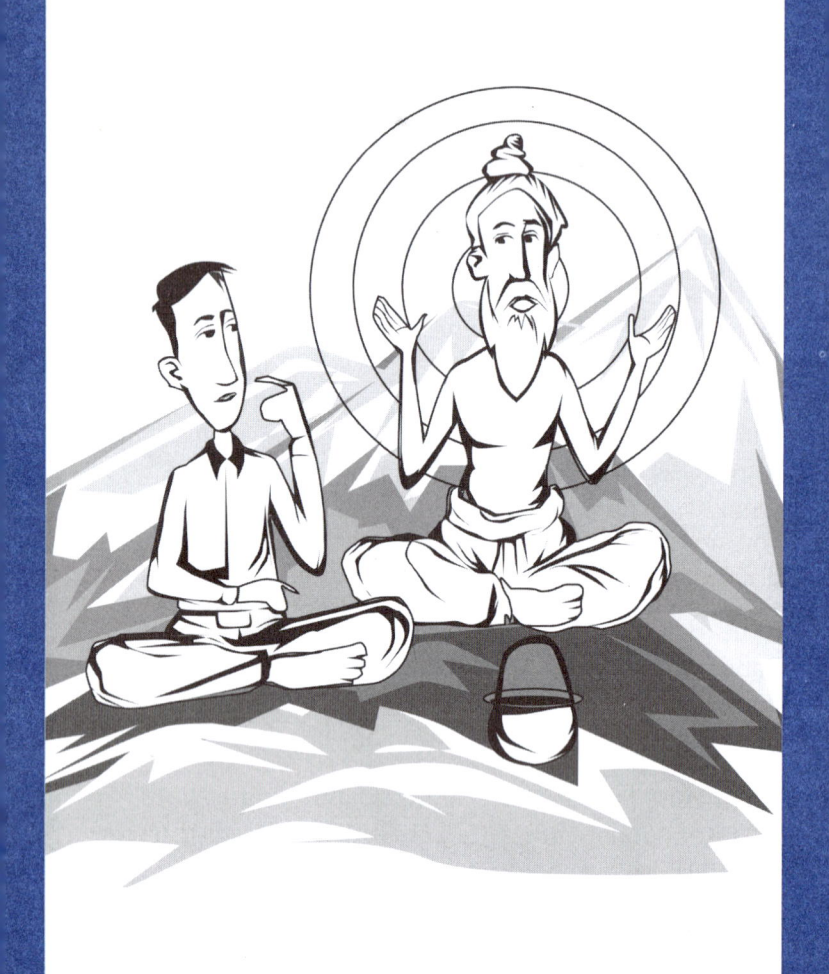

The power of forgiveness

The same holds for resentment and hurt. If someone hurts you and you carry the hurt in your mind, you are only harming yourself. The person who harmed or hurt you might have forgotten. But by carrying the hurt in your mind,

> Holding on to anger is like grasping a hot coal with the intent of throwing it at someone else; but ultimately it is you who gets burned.
>
> – *Buddha*

you continue to hurt yourself. Therefore, forgiving and forgetting is not just about pardoning the other person, but also unburdening yourself of the resentment you carry, which would otherwise keep on hurting you endlessly. It is a greater sin to keep hurting yourself by carrying resentful thoughts in your mind. Forgive and be free of the burden you are carrying. All great masters like Mahavir, Jesus and Gandhi have laid so much stress on forgiveness.

In his poem *'Go not to the temple'* the Nobel laureate poet Rabindranath Tagore says, "Go not to the temple to ask for forgiveness for your sins, first forgive from your heart those who have sinned against you."

All great spiritual teachers and philosophers of the world have over the ages stressed upon the need to forget the past hurts and to forgive those who have hurt you.

Buddhism too, when talking about compassion and kindness, lays emphasis on the ability and willingness to forgive.

When Christ was crucified, Jesus spoke from the Cross, "Lord, Forgive them for they know not what they do."

If you find it difficult to forgive others then just ask yourself – When I make a mistake don't I want others to forgive me? If the answer is yes, then why the reluctance to forgive others? Always remember that by forgiving it is you, who stand to benefit the most. Forgiveness bursts the clouds of depression, anger, frustration and resentment hanging over your mind and creates a positive energy that instills peace and calm.

Just think of the chaos in the world if everyone started to avenge the wrongs done against them.

> An eye for an eye leaves the world blind.
> – *Mahatma Gandhi*

Learning to forgive the self

Jai and Priya had been happily married for the past ten years. They were a unique couple and everyone envied their love. Jai was a successful CEO in a multinational and Priya was content taking care of her home. Suddenly, one day dark clouds overshadowed their happy life. Divya, who had been in college with Jai, turned up at their house when Jai was away, and she told Priya of their ongoing affair. Priya was shattered and she left home with her two kids to stay with her parents.

When Jai and Priya had got married, Jai had confessed about a college affair and he had told Priya about his love with Divya. What he had not told her now was the fact that he was seeing her again after so many years. Priya felt betrayed. She filed for a divorce. Jai tried to meet her several times, but she refused to see him.

Jai had broken up with Divya after college when he had come to know how materialistic she was. All she cared about was her career. He had realised that marrying her would be a mistake. She was a great lover, but she could never be a good homemaker or a mother. Jai had not kept back anything from Priya after their marriage.

Just as the first hearing for their divorce was about to come up in the court, Priya's father, who believed that Jai was innocent and had some private investigator make some investigations, left Priya aghast with a revelation. Divya had spent the past ten years building an envious career. She too was now a CEO in an MNC. And she believed that to get anything in life one has to fight for it. She had lied to Priya about the affair to break their marriage so that she could have Jai back in her life again.

Priya's father advised her to go and apologise to Jai and make up. Priya was not so sure if he would forgive her for having been so foolish and naïve. How many times he had tried to meet her? And how many times she had shut the door in his face?

But her fears were put to rest as soon as she was face to face with Jai. He hugged her before she could utter a word and said, "Priya! Don't you worry! Everything is going to be alright. I had seen through Divya's nature back then in college. That is why I broke up with her."

Priya returned to her home along with her kids and tried to get things back to normal. But it seemed that she had created a chasm that would never get filled. Guilt kept gnawing at her heart and she spent many hours crying alone. This did not escape Jai's notice and he tried his best to give her extra love and care to make her forget everything. But the more he loved her, the more the feeling of guilt seemed to strangle her heart. At last, she could take it no longer and had a nervous breakdown. She ended up in a hospital.

With the best medical care, she was discharged in a week. When she returned home, she was surprised to find that her kids were not there and the whole house was decorated just as it had been on the first night of their honeymoon.

"What is this all about?" Enquired Priya, with tears in her eyes. "Oh Jai! Don't love me so much! I do not deserve it."

Jai took her into his arms and said, "Priya! I have long forgiven you. But there is another person whose forgiveness you should seek. Till you do so, you will never be happy again."

A confused Priya looked at her husband and said, "Whose forgiveness?"

"Your own, my dear!" said Jai, "You have to forgive yourself!"

Priya burst into tears and hugged her husband. "I cannot bring myself to forgive myself," she said. "You have always been loving and I did not trust you. Rather I believed the words of a complete stranger."

"Look here," said Jai. "Suppose I had made a mistake. Would you not have forgiven me?"

"I sure would but…."

"Shhh! Then forgive yourself for my sake, for the sake of our love. Otherwise neither of us will ever be happy again. Forgive yourself for my sake, your children's sake, your happy home's sake. Do you think I have been blind to your mental state? You got ill because of your inner turmoil, guilt and forgiving yourself is the only way to release your emotional pain. Let it go now, please."

Priya understood what he was saying. She loved her husband, her kids and her home more than anything. She had dedicated the best years of her life to nurture this heaven that they called home. She could not allow it all to be blown away. She let out a sigh and lost herself in his loving arms. She was back at last! She had forgiven herself.

Life is not always paved with roses. The thorns of hurts given by others and the mistakes made by us at times make life seem like an ordeal. But we can easily step over these thorns and not allow them to keep hurting us endlessly by the magic of forgiveness. Let us remember that forgiveness is for our own sake and not for those who offended us. So learn to forgive – others and yourself too!

[Chapter Thirteen]

It comes back

"According to the Karma of past actions, one's destiny unfolds, even though everyone wants to be so lucky."
— *Sri Guru Granth Sahib*

You reap as you sow…Jaisi Karni Vaisi Bharni (whatever your actions, you have to pay likewise.)… the Law of Karma states that if you do an evil action, you are bound to suffer for it sometime or the other; and at the same time, if you do good deeds, you will likewise be rewarded for the same in the future. This law which is recognized and upheld by all the religions philosophies of the world is believed to be inescapable. It even states that no action ever goes unpaid, no matter how long it takes to manifest its result.

✯ ✯ ✯

In the battle of Mahabharat, the great warrior Bhishma fell to the arrows of Arjun. His whole body was pierced with so many arrows that when he dropped to the ground, his body was held by the arrows protruding from his back and it seemed as if he lay on a bed of arrows. Bhishma was blessed with the boon of 'death at will' and he had the power to keep his soul in his body, no matter how badly it was damaged. He lay on this bed of arrows till the end of the battle of Mahabharat, after which Lord Krishna approached him.

Upon seeing the Lord, Bhishma joined his palms and said, "O Supreme One! I have led a pious existence all along. Why do I then have to suffer thus, lying as I am with my whole body pierced with arrows?"

Lord Krishna said, "O Holy One! You well know the Law of Karma and that one has to bear with the fruit of past deeds!"

"But what did I ever do to undergo so much pain for so long?"

Upon being questioned thus, Lord Krishna used his divine power to help Bhishma peek into one of his past lives. In his past 22nd birth, Bhishma once came across a huge snake while strolling in a garden. He immediately picked a stick lying nearby, and using it, heaved the snake and threw it out of the way. The snake unfortunately landed on a thorny bush and its entire body was pierced by the long thorns. It lay writhing on the thorns for more than an hour before it died.

When Bhishma returned to the present consciousness, he said, "You are right Lord! I suffer because of my own deed. The poor snake had in no way harmed me and I was instrumental in making it suffer thus! Now I understand why I have stayed here for so many days with my body pierced with arrows."

☆ ☆ ☆

One having no faith in religion or God might consider the Law of Karma as something quite absurd. But even if one does not believe, there is someone out there keeping an account of all your deeds. One would not be able to deny that. In nature, there surely exists some law of cause and effect. When a criminal is brought to book don't we say that he is paying for his misdeed? Likewise, if we do something evil, will we not have to suffer for it some time or the other?

Good begets good

If one finds oneself suffering because of wrongs one has done, then know it that it is never too late to change the

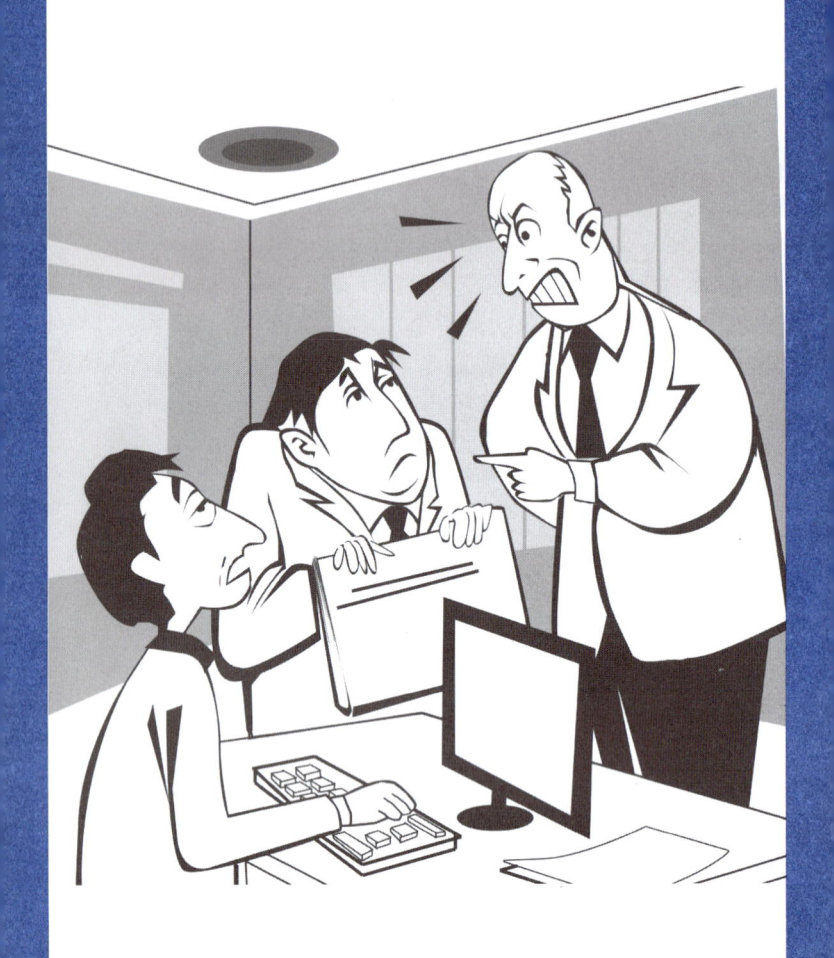

tide of things. If wrong actions have brought suffering, the right actions could well change things and lead you to joy and peace.

★ ★ ★

There was a very successful businessman, but he was ruthless and devoid of any feelings. All he cared for was to earn more and more. He drove his employees with an iron hand. Every person who worked for him would always be under tension and anxiety. He would not relax for a moment or allow anyone to relax. He demanded results and got them, no matter how. If anyone asked for a break or a day off, he would just fire that person. He worked 16 hours a day and more, and forced others to work with him. He never had a vacation or even a holiday himself and totally neglected his relations who tried to get in touch with him.

Such was his drive that he had built an enviable business empire, worth billions of dollars. One day, around the age of fifty, he was diagnosed with cancer. And the tests declared that he had a very short time to live – three months at the most! It was like a bolt of lightning! He was shocked to know that nothing, whether his wealth or power could save him. And for the first time in his life, he sat down totally helpless and relaxed. He realised that in the race to earn more and more, he had not even enjoyed life. All he had given to himself as well as to others was tension. This was the driving force that had made him achieve so much. But to what end?

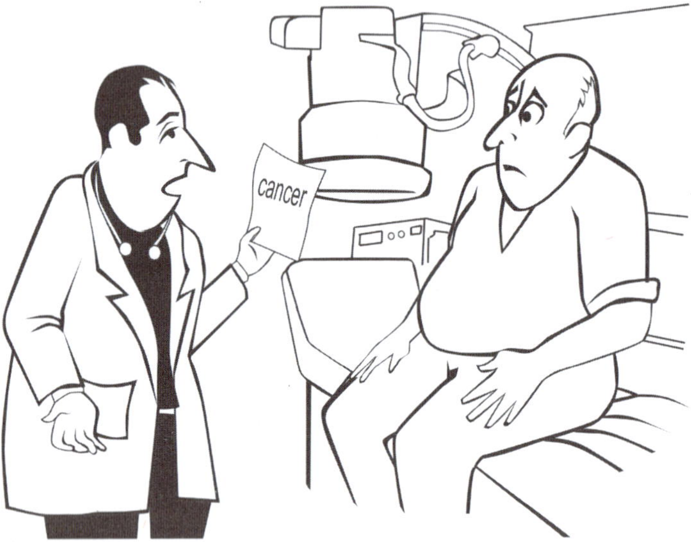
cancer

It seemed to him that the tension he had nurtured all his life had now taken the form of the dreaded disease. He had not allowed himself even simple pleasures and any happiness in life. As this realization dawned upon him, he decided enough was enough. He called up his lawyers and had all his assets liquidated. He made generous gifts to friends and relatives, whom he did not even like to meet earlier. He also donated generously to charitable causes. Having given away more than two thirds of his wealth, one day he quietly left the city without informing anyone.

He travelled aimlessly and after several weeks reached a small village in the mountains. This beautiful hamlet was virtually cut off from the rest of the world. He was struck by the beauty and serenity of the place and decided to stay there for some time. There were hardly fifty families living there. Very soon he befriended all of them, especially the kids. No one knew who he was.

All day long he would walk through the mountains, play with the children and just enjoy life. He soon realized that the place had no school. So he started teaching the kids. He got so involved in social activities that he did not know how time went by, till one fine day he suddenly remembered the prophecy of the doctors.

Next day he went back to the city and had the tests done again. The doctors were pleasantly surprised that he had shown tremendous improvement. He returned to the village and spent the rest of his days in community work caring for others. Whereas, greed, lack of compassion, a tense life had led him to the brink of death; charity, love and compassion gave him a new lease of life.

☆ ☆ ☆

Remember what you give to life, life gives the same back to you! If tension, worry, anger are your feelings, life will be equally harsh towards you. And if you try to dispense love, care and compassion, life will make you happy and joyful! The Law of Karma does not just mean how you treat others or behave with others. It also implies how you treat yourself.

What you give comes back!

If you sow chilly seeds, you can hardly expect apples!

We reap what we sow. Any good or bad we do, will come back to us. Not only doing, even thoughts too have energy – positive or negative. We must think before we do something bad to another person. If someone does mean to us, it is his karma. We should not react, instead let it go.

Whenever thoughts of anger, revenge and hatred come, simply tell yourself, "I do not want to think this way." Let us remember that every negative emotion or act makes us devoid of the tremendous energy of love and love is like "glue", which unites us and gives tremendous happiness.

Can we change our Karma?

Karma is a word used very often. But do we try to remember the Law of Karma to make our life better and happier.

Karma relates not just to actions, but also to our thoughts. Thoughts are the primary energy, which later culminate into action. This energy can be positive or negative. If one thinks positively, positive things happen and if one thinks negatively, negative things take place. It therefore implies that if one thinks evil of someone, without actually doing anything evil, one generates Karma. In other words, one generates a negative energy which might or might not harm the other person, but certainly harms the thinker creating mental disturbances.

So, if we wish to "turn around our karma", it has to begin with our thoughts. One has to think positive and good. Even if someone has wronged you, be careful of what you think or do, because consequences will be yours.

> How people treat you is their karma; how you react is yours.
> – Wayne Dyer

If you are angry at someone because he has been mean to you, anger may or may not harm that person, but it will surely do you no good, physically or mentally. Learn to forgive. It isn't easy, but try.

Develop a method of self-correction. Check your feelings, your thoughts, your mindful machinations; you will find that with practice, your mind will learn

> Thought materialises and becomes an action. If you allow the mind to dwell on good, elevating thoughts, you will do naturally good and laudable actions.
> – Swami Sivanand

to filter the negativities and focus only on the positive.

> Love conquers everything even Karma.
> – Julien Offray de La Mettrie

Another very potent means of turning around the Karma is love! Remember, it is the energy of love that holds mankind together.

From the fountain of love, only positive feelings and thoughts can spring forth. When we sow positivity and love, we get back the same from life. In other words, by planting love, we are able to harvest love for ourselves!

Moreover, the act of loving is an act of letting go of your ego. This is because in love, one thinks of others, rather than the self.

In essence, the key to going beyond the stranglehold of the Law of Karma is constituted by three things – forgiveness, love and positive thinking. Let everyone know it…let us spread the good karma.

[Chapter Fourteen]

Reshape ... Remake Yourself

"As human beings, our greatness lies not so much in being able to remake the world – that is the myth of the atomic age – as in being able to remake ourselves."

— *Mahatma Gandhi*

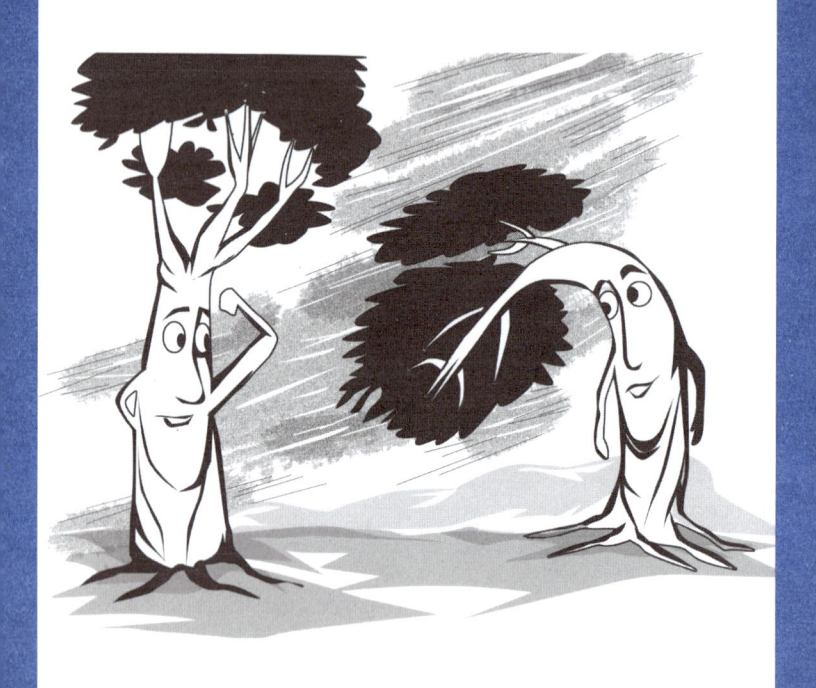

There is the fable of two trees that grew adjacent to each other. One was proud and rigid, and it stood up straight and stoic. The other had a flexible trunk that made it sway to the breeze in every direction. The first tree would often say, "You are no match when it comes to strength. Even a gust of wind can make you bow. Look at me! I can stand up straight even in a storm! No one can make me bow!"

The other tree would silently listen to the first tree's proud words. One day, there was a storm like never before. It seemed that the fury of hell had been unleashed. The flexible tree was bent over till the tip kissed the ground. It adapted itself to the circumstance and just snuggled close to the earth waiting for the storm to abate. When the storm ended, the flexible tree slowly straightened up and looked around. Where was its friend?

It saw the rigid tree lying uprooted some distance away!

☆ ☆ ☆

This storm is a metaphor for life's problems and adversities. People who are flexible and ready to reshape themselves

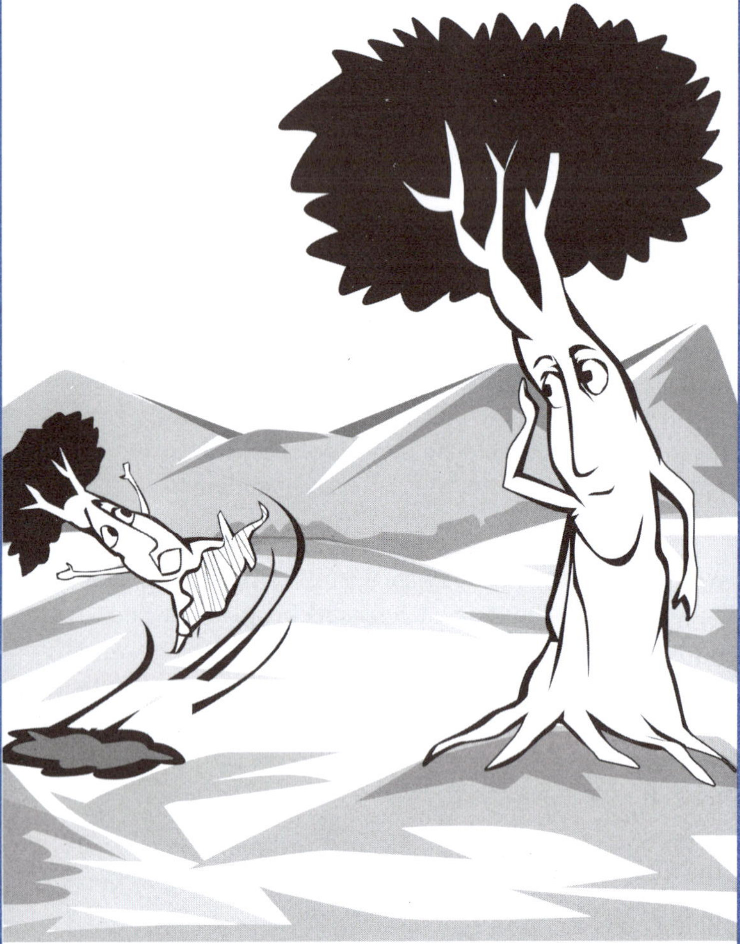

according to the circumstances survive and come out triumphant. On the other hand, those who remain rigid suffer and end up defeated.

Reshaping or changing according to the circumstances, however, does not imply giving in to pressures. It means making use of those circumstances for personal growth! Each adversity that appears in life brings in an opportunity for us to reshape ourselves for a better and happy future. If you change, you progress and thrive. If you don't, chances are that you would stagnate and make no progress.

Many a times, life seems unfair. The brave, take each setback as a chance to reshape themselves and try for higher accomplishments. To the mind it would seem foolhardiness if a person went on trying even after repeated setbacks and failures. But there has been someone who reshaped and remade himself to become a lighthouse for millions.

After he was twenty three years old, he had separated from his father, he studied English grammar – imperfectly, but so as to speak and write. For the most part of his life, he taught himself. Self education, determination and an indomitable spirit took him to the levels of success, unparalleled in the history of mankind.

Being politically ambitious, between the age of twenty-nine and forty-nine, he

> Wisdom is not a product of schooling, but of the life-long attempt to acquire it. Learn from yesterday, live for today, hope for tomorrow. The important thing is, to not stop questioning.
>
> – *Albert Einstein*

lost seven elections. Now what if he had given up? – Would he, at fifty-one been elected as the President of the United State of America. The man was Abraham Lincoln. His attitude towards the repeated failures is reflected in what he once said: "I am a slow walker, but I never walk back."

★ ★ ★

At a senior position in a company, I was a member of the interviewing and recruitment board. Of all the interactions, I had over the years I distinctly remember two very vividly. In a single day, we had hired two highly capable engineers.

Everyone on the interview board was impressed with their merit and had no doubts about their capabilities. They started working with the company and impressed everyone. Personally at the initial stages, I too was sure that both of them would rise high on the ladder, but as time passed I had to change my opinion about one of them.

Both were equally talented and intelligent, but while one was open to ideas from others and would readily adapt to circumstances and suggestions given by his teammates, the other was rather headstrong and would not be willing to relent from the stand he had once taken. Sometime later, I moved from that company to another, and many years down the line, I ran into a senior management member from my old company. I happened to ask about the two bright engineers and was least surprised when I learnt that while the first one had managed to climb up the management ladder and was now the Vice President, the other one was still, just a manager!

★ ★ ★

This and many other examples from life have taught that life is nothing but a series of changes! In fact that is the true definition of life – change!

How Life Reshapes Us Constantly

Look around and you will find things changing all the time in nature too! That is what makes it progressive, vibrant and alive, otherwise it would be nothing more than a stagnant existence.

> Man must reshape himself through the power of the will; and having lifted himself, he should never let himself be dragged down. For this self, alone is your friend and indeed, this self alone is your enemy.
> – *Lord Krishna in The Bhagavad Gita*

Science has also taught us that even the so-called inanimate objects are undergoing subtle changes all the time! Nothing in fact is static and reshaping goes on endlessly!

Life's greatest achievement, if one asks, is to continuously reshape and remake oneself so that there is optimum growth and we can live life happily.

During the journey of life, life does throw many challenges at us, giving opportunities to us to learn and remake ourselves. Problems in life actually give us a chance to grow.

To begin with, as children, we are fed the ideals of honesty, truth, sincerity, friendship and so on, whether by the family, society or our education. We firmly believe in these ideals and dream of upholding the same in all the circumstances of life. As kids therefore, we are taught to imagine a utopian world, where all wrongs can be made right by adhering to these high ideals. Some of us even attempt to make the society, the nation and the world a perfect place through our idealism.

As we emerge from the safe sanctuaries of our homes, to fend for ourselves in the outside world, we get to meet different people. Then our perspective undergoes a dramatic change; when we encounter lies, deceit and corruption. Either we become one among the pack or we resist. It is only when we resist, that character takes birth. It is here that a conflict and turmoil starts within us; between our earlier beliefs and the new scenario.

Some of us turn to books and gurus for guidance and inspiration. We let the struggle become a part of us, with inspiration from speakers and writers – "never give up", "hard times do not last but hard people do", "remain positive in each circumstance". This is when some of us, who continue optimistically and through self education and reshaping, are able to make a mark in their world.

Moreover, right from our childhood, we are told by our parents, teachers, lecturers and the society around us what to think, what to do and how to behave. Based on our environment and family patterns, we are conditioned to think, behave and act in a certain manner – religiously, socially and economically. In other words, our upbringing, our teaching, our books and our society tell us "what to think" and not "how to think".

Remember, teachers, parents and others can only show us the way; but it is we and we alone, who have to travel it. We therefore need to free ourselves from the fixed patterns of behaviour and conditioning to go beyond those barriers. Many people, young or old, like this conditioning and choose to live in that world. They dare not go beyond. They are afraid of what their parents, friends, relations would say and how the society would react. They continue to hold the barriers around them, while some question, watch themselves and never thoughtlessly accept what they are told. Rather, they always investigate, think, unlearn, learn, unlearn and keep learning all the time. They are firm believers that for self development, they must strive themselves.

For better or worse, life is never like a track of railway lines which always goes along a fixed route. Rather life makes ways in impossible directions. It forces one to think, change one's perspective to continually remake and reshape oneself.

☆ ☆ ☆

The same happened with a young man in the early twentieth century. He was educated in law from England and was dreaming of a career in law. That was the course his life was taking in South Africa, when one day, something happened that completely changed his life and along with it, the destiny of his country. He bought a first class train ticket and got into the designated compartment. At another station, a white man boarded the train and seeing that a non-white was travelling in a first class compartment, became very upset. He summoned a railway official, who asked the young man to move out of the compartment.

When he protested, he was thrown out of the compartment along with his baggage by a constable. The incident changed the course of his life. Something snapped within the young man and he resolved to protest against racial discrimination. He launched a campaign to end discrimination against the Indians in South Africa and the method of non-violent protest he adopted made him quite famous, so much so that when he returned to his own country, India, he was welcomed like a hero and thus was born in him the dream to free his people from the British rule.

This man, Mahatma Gandhi, was forced by circumstances to reshape his thinking and dream of freedom from foreign rule. The dream to set his people free was born when he himself found his own freedom at stake. It was an impractical dream – to take on the entire British Empire – and a very difficult and extraordinary goal. But such was the impact of the incident on Gandhi's mind that his whole perspective underwent a sea change; and a law graduate became focused on fighting for the rights of his people.

Lord Buddha once said, "As an irrigator guides water to the fields, as the archer aims an arrow, as a carpenter carves a piece of wood, the wise men shape their lives." Life threw a gauntlet in Gandhi's face and like a wise man he used this opportunity to reshape the course of his life and rewrite history by remaking the destiny of his people and country.

While everyone, who has heard or read about Abraham Lincoln or Mahatma Gandhi knows of their successes and great achievements, one completely ignores the failures and setbacks that they had to face, which actually played an important role in reshaping their personalities.

Reshape & Remake

> A few kilograms of iron ore costs around Rs 50.
> A bar of iron costs around Rs 500.
> The same bar moulded in any form costs around Rs 1500.
> And made into springs, doors, needles costs in thousands of rupees.
> And made into automobile steel, special steels costs in lakhs of rupees.

What does it prove?

Your value is determined by what you can make of yourself and not by what you are.

Life is like a classroom full of tests, trials, as well as lessons. The only attribute that the student needs, is the openness to learn. Learning helps one grow. Learning helps one reshape one's thinking. Learning opens up new avenues of opportunities. Frankly, the day you stop learning, you are as good as dead!

It need not be a skill or a newly acquired degree. Reshaping our consciousness / our mind, modifying our attitudes, our thoughts, our perspectives irrespective of our past or present circumstances will always inch towards a brighter and better future.

> ALWAYS EXPECT MORE FROM YOURSELF THAN FROM OTHERS; BECAUSE EXPECTATIONS FROM OTHERS HURT A LOT, WHILE EXPECTATIONS FROM SELF INSPIRE A LOT.

William Butler Yeats, the Irish poet, once wrote –

> *The friends that have I do it wrong,*
> *whenever I remake a song,*
> *Should know what issue is at stake:*
> *It is myself that I remake.*

[Chapter Fifteen]

Accept Life as it Comes

"God, grant me the serenity to accept the things I cannot change, the courage to change the things I can, and the wisdom to know the difference."

– *Reinhold Niebuhr*

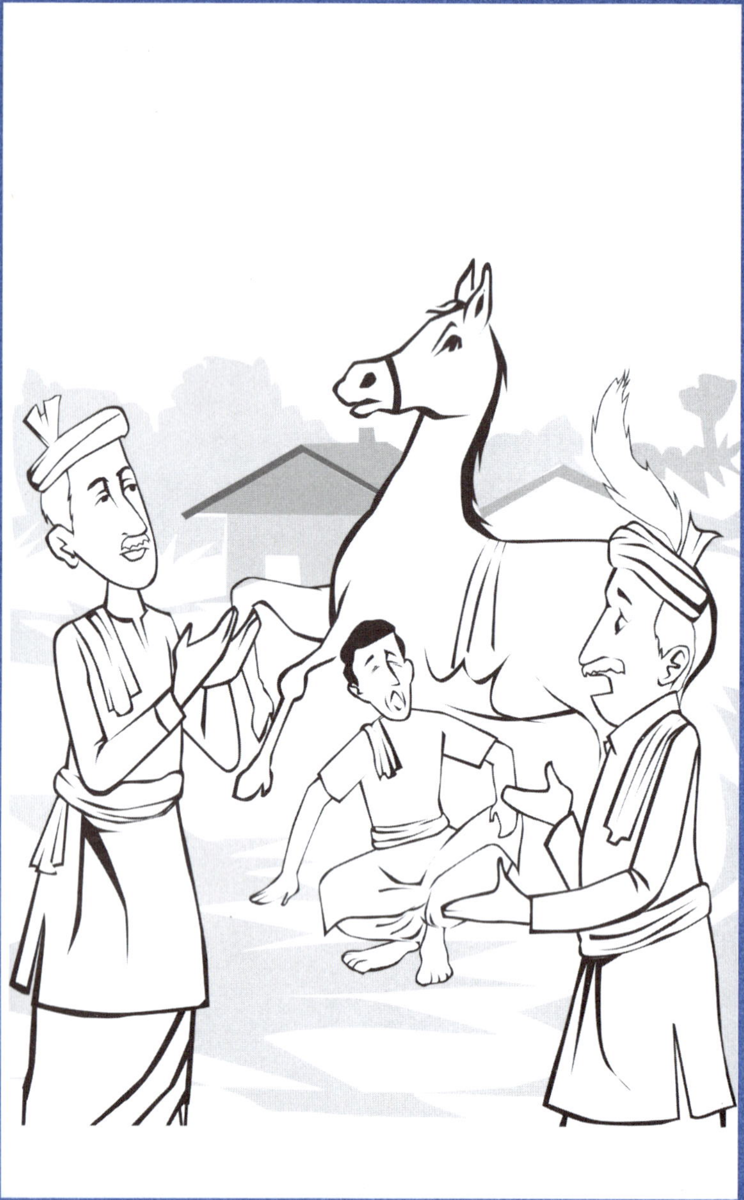

There lived a farmer who had learnt to take life in its stride. One day, his neighbour came running and said, "What are you doing? Your horse has run away!"

The farmer showed no signs of getting perturbed and calmly said, "As God wills! Don't worry. He will come back."

The following morning, the farmer saw his horse near the stable with three other horses from the nearby forest. The neighbour also happened to turn up at the same moment, and remarked with surprise, "Your horse has come back! And where did these three other horses come from? Seems they followed your horse from the forest! That is what I call luck!"

The farmer just said, "As God wills!"

The same day, the farmer's son tried to ride one of the wild horses. The horse baulked and threw him off! The boy broke his leg and had to be plastered. Seeing the boy's plight, the ever so talkative neighbour said, "These wild horses are not lucky at all! Look your son has broken his leg."

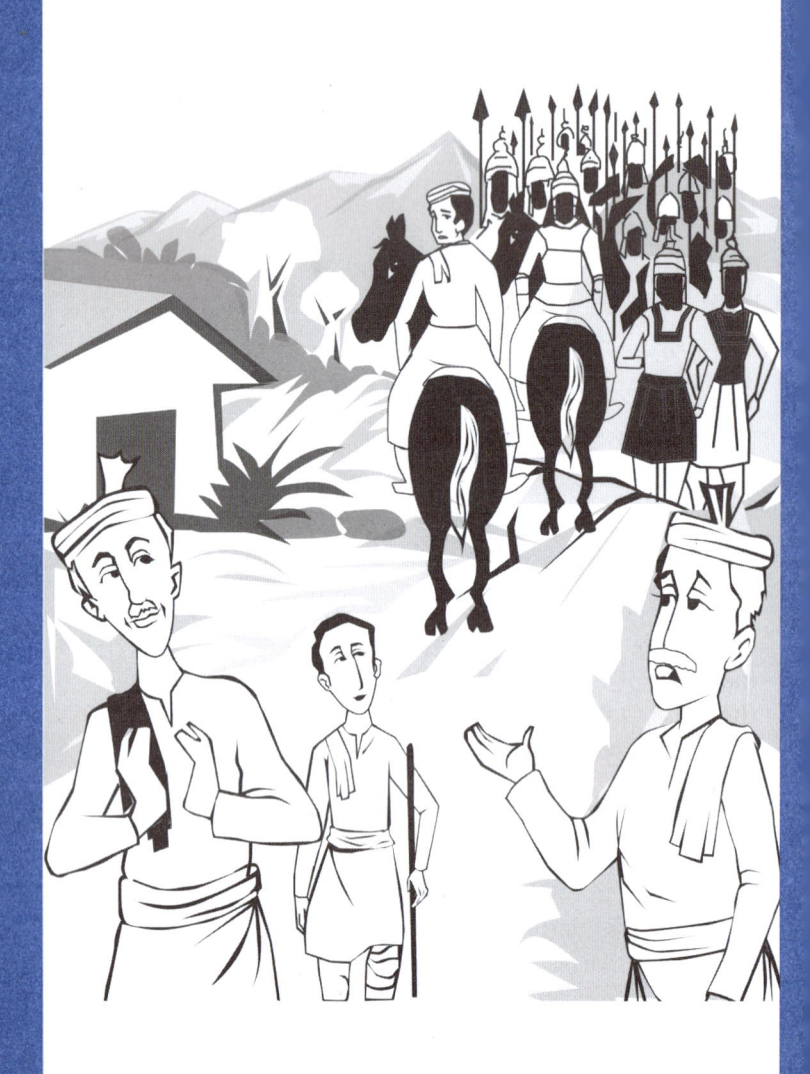

The farmer still remained calm and said, "As God wills!"

A few days later, the neighbouring king declared a war against their kingdom. Army officers turned up at the village to recruit young men into the army. When they saw the broken leg of the farmer's son, they rejected him. The neighbour's young son however, was selected and he had to go along. At this, the neighbour said, "If he had not broken his leg, he would have had to go to war! This proved lucky for him."

Again all the farmer said was, "As God wills!"

☆ ☆ ☆

The farmer's attitude towards life is what most religions and philosophies around the world preach – Accept God's will! Though some people believe that one can control everything in life, if we delve deeper, we would realise that there are events and happenings in life that are beyond our control. And if that is so, it is advisable to accept the inevitable rather than fret and fume, or try and go against the tide.

Remember: **Pursuing desires and goals, which are unrealistic, will lead to stress, tension, frustration and unhappiness.**

Gurbani says, *"Sahaj subah jo hoai, so ho"* – whatever happens is naturally the best. When we fall in line with our karmic destiny, life is lived effortlessly.

Understand life

How happy we would be if we understood and accepted the stark realities of life. The inevitable and the unchangeable should not be our focus. If we just ponder, life in its present form is something we never demanded. We never requested. We never asked for. We did not ask to be born dark or fair, poor or rich, tall or short, part of this family or that. In other words, we did not choose our birth or the circumstances of our birth. It is there as a gift from God, without our asking for it, and we accept it, because we cannot change it; whereas certain situations in life, those too given by God, we choose not to accept, depending upon our thought process.

This does not imply that we should not work or make any effort. We must work; we must put our best efforts but they should be productive.

> No matter what you do, life turns out the way it turns out. Struggling with life does not help at all.
>
> – Osho

☆ ☆ ☆

Randy Pausch, the professor at Carnegie Mellon University inspired thousands of students in the classroom and countless people worldwide through his highly acclaimed "last lecture". He died of pancreatic cancer at the age of 47. Pausch, who had a remarkable sense of humour, began his lecture by pulling up on an overhead screen a trio of CAT scans that showed the ten tumors in his liver and spoke about his doctor's prognosis that he had three to six months of good health left.

"That is what it is," he simply said. "We cannot change it. We cannot change the cards we are dealt – just how we play the hand."

He went on to speak about brick-walls that often appear in the path of every accomplishment. "Remember," he said, "The brick-walls are there for a reason. The brick-walls are not there to keep us out. The brick-walls are there to give us a chance to show how badly we want something. The brick-walls are there to stop the people who don't want it badly enough."

By sharing his personal ordeal, Pausch taught us how to accept life as it comes, by effectively using our infinite talent, strength and energy that resides within each one of us.

☆ ☆ ☆

An old woman lost her only son. She carried his body to Lord Buddha, as she had heard that he had divine powers. She fell at his feet and in the most piteous manner asked him for the life of her son. When Lord Buddha saw that no words could console the old woman, he sent her on a futile hunting spree and said, "Fine old mother! I will revive your son. But for that, you will have to go to a house where no one has ever died and bring me the dust from its floor."

The old woman got up at once and left. She hopefully went to every door in her village, but found that every family had lost someone, some time. Still, she was not disheartened. She rushed to the adjoining village and then the next.

At last, after wandering from house to house for days, she realised what Buddha was trying to convey to her. Death spares none! Everyone has to die one day or the other. Even if her son was to come back to life, one day he would surely die again! She realised that right from the time we take the first breath, our journey towards the grave begins.

☆ ☆ ☆

Death is the saddest truth of life. At the same time, death is an integral part of life. One who is unwilling to die, cannot live. Accepting it is sure to lessen some fear associated with it. Why fear something that is bound to happen. It is the law.

Leading a better life comes with accepting the laws of living. One such law is that life is an intermittent game of joys and sorrows. Life plays hide and seek with joys. If it finds good phases, at times it encounters bad patches too; that's when joy is in the hiding! It's a pity that sometimes the bad patches come in spite of our best efforts. In such times, it is useless to lose one's cool. We should adopt the attitude of the farmer who accepted each happening as the will of God. Little do we know then that an event we might think as unlucky may eventually turn out in our favour.

☆ ☆ ☆

A powerful and famous English noble's fourteen-year-old son got trapped in a bog while hunting. Luckily, he was rescued by a farmer and the nobleman was relieved to find his son was safe. This was not the end of their harrowing experience but the beginning of another story.

What happened next proved instrumental in saving the life of the noble's son yet again when he got seriously ill years later. As the thankful noble was leaving with his son, he happened to see the farmer's son, who was just as old as his own son. Out of gratitude, the nobleman offered to take the farmer's son with him to the city and get him educated. The farmer gladly accepted the kind proposal.

The farmer's son excelled in his studies and graduated in medicine from a medical school in London. He also went on to make a remarkable discovery that revolutionized the field of medicine. Some years later, the nobleman's son contracted pneumonia and was in a serious condition. But the discovery of the young doctor saved him! This young doctor was none other than Sir Alexander Fleming who discovered Penicillin, the nobleman was Lord Randolph Churchill and his son who was saved by Fleming's drug was none other than Sir Winston Churchill.

☆ ☆ ☆

Strange stories happen in strange ways. Life weaves its intricate events. If Winston Churchill was not caught in the bog as a boy and later saved by Fleming's father, his son would never have become a doctor and probably not discovered Penicillin. And Winston Churchill would have lost his life to pneumonia. Who could say that the accidental act of getting trapped in mire would prove so fortuitous for so many?

Our will versus our destiny

Life is like a wild river that meanders and flows along many courses but never follows a set path. Usually, we do not understand this. What we understand is that we have to pursue our goals and aspirations, some of which are formed because of our parent's wishes, some that are the result of our social conditioning and then some as a result of our education. Destiny might surprise us with a different plan altogether. What happens in the process is a tug of war between what is destined for us and what we want as our destiny. The outcome is unsatisfactory if destiny wins and if we don't, we could end up like a square peg in a round hole.

An avid music lover aspires to be a musician, but because he has been told that the profession of a doctor is more profitable, he might be compelled towards the latter. He might succeed as a doctor, but he would never be satisfied within. Think for a moment: Amitabh Bachchan started his career as an executive in a company. The hard working man that he is, he would surely have made a success out of that career too. But would he have achieved the same name and fame had he not followed the calling of his heart?

One thing about life is that it moves and unfolds in strange ways. In order to get the maximum out of it, discard all preconceived notions. Accepting life as it unfolds can bring amazing levels of happiness and contentment.

> We must let go of the life we have planned, so as to accept the one that is waiting for us.
> – *Joseph Campbell*

Believing and accepting that pleasures and pains, happiness and unhappiness are a part and parcel of our existence can help us to sail through life smoothly. On the other hand, trying to defy or struggle against the blows that life chooses to give could fill us up with a kind of negative energy. When we choose to go with the flow and accept life as it comes, we gain deeper insight that enables us to overcome the frustration, the anger and the bitterness.

Remember, when in trouble, never complain against life or you'll double the troubles for yourself. Cribbing leads to bitterness, which in turn adversely affects the mental and physical health. 'Why me' attitude only exerts your choice over the inevitable phase that you are destined to live.

On the other hand, going along with the flow will give you the experience that pleasure and pain are but two sides of the same coin. Trying to fight against this reality will only worsen things for you.

> Don't choose. Accept life as it is in its totality.
> – *Osho*

How to accept life as it is?

Tough as it may seem for discussion, many people feel it is an act of cowardice to accept things as they are in life. In reality, accepting things as they are in fact requires tremendous inner strength and courage! It also requires a lot of faith in the power that we call God! And this act of faith in its turn requires humility. Acceptance is humility, for you bow to the high command!

"Jehi Viddhi Rakhe Ram, Tehi Viddhi Rahiye" means that I accept the will of God and live by it!

The all omnipotent, the divine power – exists! It is through His grace that we have got life and it is through His grace that we go along in it each moment. Fundamental to the process of acceptance of life on its own terms is expressing one's appreciation for God. This attitude enriches our value system and keeps all frustration, complaints, irritants and negativity away from us. It not only proves to be a way of enjoyment but also emotionally detaches us from all happenings especially tragedies that otherwise fill people with fear. That fear emanates pain and suffering in life, thus making such moments all the more unbearable and intolerable.

> The only way to live is to accept each minute as an unrepeatable miracle, which is exactly what it is: a miracle and unrepeatable.
> *– Storm Jameson*

Every day, every hour, every minute, every second is a miracle, irrespective of whether it brings pleasure or pain! A miracle of life gifted by God! And the best way to go about is to accept what falls to one's share with a song on our lips, dancing to the notes of life! Life is in itself the means and an end; the journey and the destination! It is an experience unparalleled, very beautifully expounded by the Indian poet and Noble laureate, Rabindranath Tagore.

"These paper boats of mine are meant to dance on the ripples of hours, and not reach any destination."

[Chapter Sixteen]

Ultimate Relationship

"You can kiss your family and friends good-bye and put miles between you, but at the same time you carry them with you in your heart, your mind … because you don't just live in a world but a world lives in you."

– *Frederick Buechner*

"Our greatest joy and our greatest pain comes in our relationships with others."

– *Stephen R. Covey*

No person can live in isolation. Therefore, life is a relationship. Life cannot be without a relationship. We live only in relationship.

Our personality is interwoven with relationships. Even in the animal and plant kingdoms, there exist relationships that play a pivotal role in survival and existence. To deny these relationships is like denying existence.

Every human being has a deep seated urge to get connected, to look for relationship. There are contributing relationships and there are detrimental or painful relationships. Each one is there for a reason. While one may help us achieve, the other may help us to develop and evolve. On the whole, whether good or bad – all relationships are there to help us progress in life!

✔ The right basis of relationships

Relationships are based on dependence, whether you depend on someone or someone depends on you. This dependence may be emotional, social, psychological, creative, financial or economical in nature. Often the basis of relationship rests with the fulfillment of this need and determines our happiness. Such dependence can lead to fear, doubt, possessiveness and insecurity. What, if the need is not fulfilled?

Most relationships are a paradoxical mess. Take marriage for instance. A marriage is an institution. But the truth is not all make it an institution. We have all heard of demanding relationships, stressful relationships. Can there be a "No-demand" relationship? The answer is Yes.

> ...most people enter a relationship in order to get something. They're trying to find someone who's going to make them feel good. In reality, the only way a relationship will last is if you see your relationship as a place that you go to give, and not a place that you go to take.
> – *AnthonyRobbins*

True relationship implies relating without any fear, pre-conditions or demands, understanding each other and communicating freely. Is a husband-wife relationship just a communion? Perhaps physically yes, but that is not relationship. In a true relationship, there is love and not duty; and love for each other exceeds the expectation from each other. A relationship can flower only when there is unconditional love.

> A loving relationship is one in which the loved one is free ... to laugh with me, but never at me; to cry with me, but never because of me; to love life, to love himself, to love being loved.
> – *Leo F. Buscaglia*

Then what if this loved one leaves you, what if one dies?

Where does the love go? Does the relationship end in bereavement?

The relationships in the world do not last long because we try to search for love in others. This is the wrong way to go about because the real source of love is within. Ever heard the great gurus of the world telling you – know thyself! They are not bluffing you know. Self knowledge is the beginning to understanding and maintaining relationship.

> ...we're always searching for somebody to complete us. When... we find that we're still unfulfilled, we blame our partners and take up with somebody more promising. This can go on ... until we admit that while a partner can add sweet dimensions to our lives, we, each of us, are responsible for our own fulfillment. Nobody else can provide it for us, and to believe otherwise is to delude ourselves ...
> – *Tom Robbins*

Once an inner relationship is established with the soul within, the fountain of divine love will flow effortlessly and automatically. When you are aware of the self, love comes in the relationship automatically.

Moreover, in any relationship, one is constantly revealing one's own personality. A jealous projection of love reveals a weak, insecure human being from within who's personality gets projected in the relationship. The solution is to meditate and tap into the power of the soul, where the most potent element is only love…some even call this divine within – God i.e. God in You and You in God.

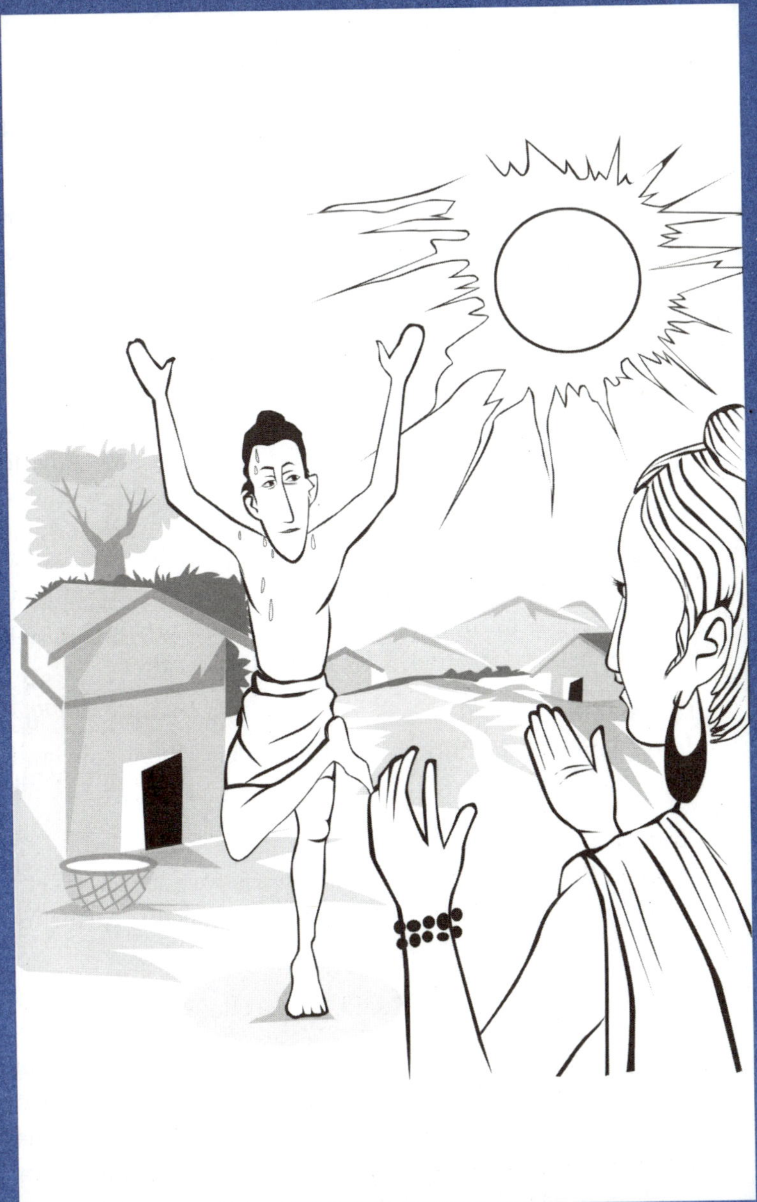

This process can be amorphous and often like searching in the dark, but with patience and perseverance, success is certain.

If Jesus was able to forgive those who crucified him, it was because he had established the ultimate relationship with the God within. If Mother Teresa could selflessly devote her entire life for the poor and sick, it was because she was with the divine, from which love flowed limitlessly. Remember, human feelings are limited and they can bring only limited love in life. But oneness with one's divine self is a source of unlimited love.

Once, while travelling through a village, Buddha came across an ascetic standing on one foot in the harsh summer sun and performing severe penance. Buddha approached him and asked, "Brother, why do you suffer thus?"

The ascetic said, "I see so many people in pain. I am doing penance to find a way to alleviate their pain and suffering."

"But you are torturing the self within. You and the self are one! By torturing the body you are torturing the self! How can you end the suffering of others by torturing yourself?"

"Then what should I do?" said the ascetic.

"Your thought of helping others is very pious. I can feel your love for others," said Buddha. "But this love is not enough. To be able to help others you need to know the self! The self is the source of divine love and it is this love

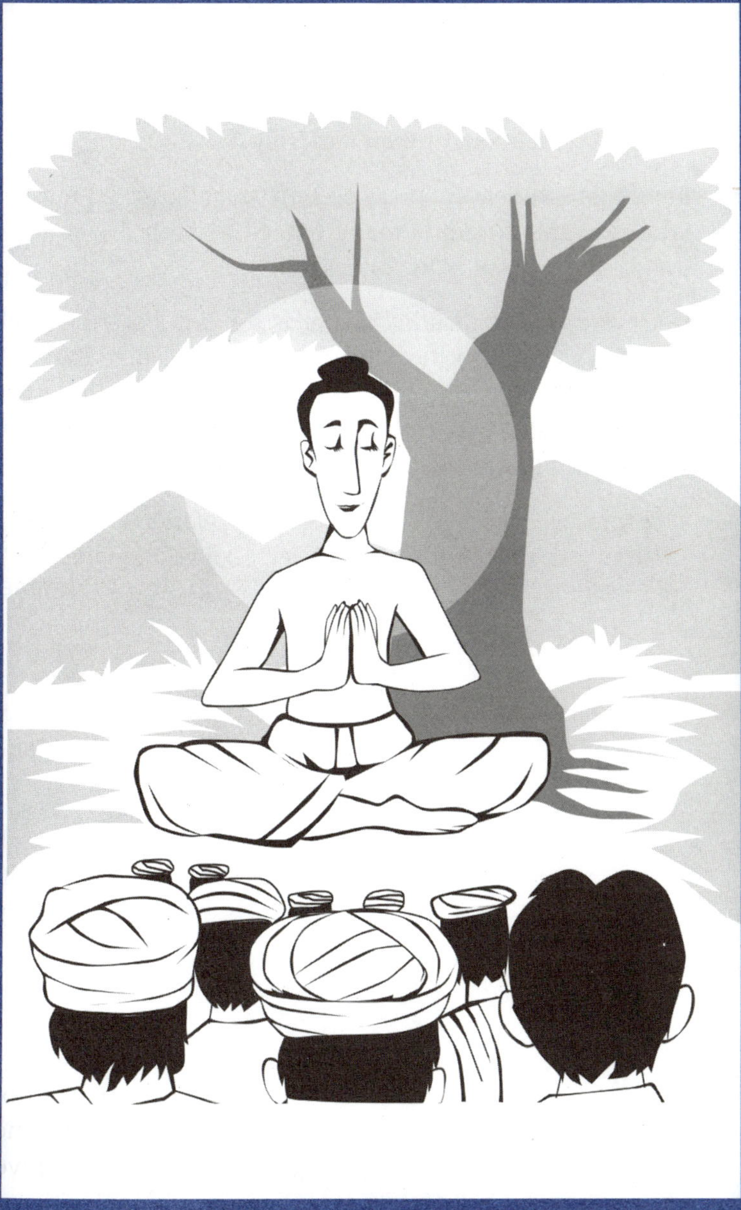

alone that can help you relate with the people in the world and guide them out of their suffering."

Later this ascetic went on to become an enlightened master who was able to guide many others through divine love that he discovered in his own self.

Jesus and Buddha said, "Master is the link between God and You" Going to the Master makes us realize that we are one and there is no separation. Let us try to be in touch with the Master. Having achieved this, we begin relating to our self and that is the ultimate relationship.

> "Before we can have a successful relationship with anyone, we first need a perfect personal relationship."
> – *Russ Von Hoelscher*